T0107184

THE SCIENCE OF GETTING RICH

THE SCIENCE OF GETTING RICH

WITH STUDY GUIDE
BY THERESA PUSKAR

WALLACE D. WATTLES

MEDIA

MEDIA

Published 2018 by Gildan Media LLC
aka G&D Media
www.GandDmedia.com

FIRST EDITION 2018

Front Cover design by David Rheinhardt of Pyrographx

Interior design by Meghan Day Healey of Story Horse, LLC

Library of Congress Cataloging-in-Publication Data is available upon request

ISBN: 978-1-7225-0006-1

10 9 8 7 6 5 4 3 2 1

Contents

Note from the Study Guide Author

Congratulations! You have just embarked on a remarkable journey of self-discovery and personal fulfillment. While the tenets of *The Science of Getting Rich* are not new, they touch on a universal truth that has withstood the test of time. More recently referred to as *The Law of Attraction*, *The Science of Getting Rich* has taken many committed followers to great heights, both professionally and personally. Wallace Wattles stood at the forefront of these living truths and is in fact, considered by many as their originator. As one of the first in the world to publish a book on the psychology of getting rich, he was most certainly an innovator and pioneer during his time. If you follow the instructions that he outlines throughout this revolutionary book, and fully commit to the program he has created, you may find your life shifting in ways you never dreamed possible.

After several years of working in the motivational world, and having heard the tenets outlined in this book for decades, I still find myself struck by the power of Wattles' writing. There is something that is extraordinary in the way in which he shares his insights and directives. While it is difficult to pinpoint exactly what makes this book so deeply motivating, it most certainly has an energy that is powerful and tangible. Perhaps through his own dedication, faith, unyielding commitment to and gratitude for the success of this book, he has modeled and molded the science into this manifestation of a classic that will undoubtedly impact your life in the extraordinary way that it has mine.

The study guide segments are structured with introspective questions that will allow you to explore your inner world, and apply the wisdom the author imparts to your life. Be sure to take the time to thoroughly study this book. Read through Wallace Wattles' pioneering text several times, allowing it to infiltrate both your conscious and sub-conscious mind. Commit yourself to completing the study guide segments as well. Taking the suggested action steps listed in the study guide will turn basic learning exercises into transformative action-based applications.

You will soon discover that while many have followed in Wattles' footsteps, the lessons he teaches and the care with which he communicates his message are very compelling. That being said, you will find a great deal of repetitiveness throughout *The Science of Getting Rich* book and accompanying study guide. This repetition is a conscious and deliberate choice made by the authors. Emphasizing and re-emphasizing philosophies and practices, so that you will both consciously and subconsciously integrate their wisdom into every cell of your being, is integral to the success of this process. You will note that as you follow the instructions suggested throughout Wattles' book and this accompanying manual, the specifics of your dreams, the contents of your visions, and the insights you gain will shift and change. As you grow, so will your desires. I encourage you to see each exercise as a new opportunity to redefine your dreams and reactivate your energy. Enjoy this journey of rejuvenation and self-discovery and believe!

Theresa Puskar
Study Guide Author

Preface

This book is pragmatical, not philosophical; a practical manual, not a treatise upon theories. It is intended for the men and women whose most pressing need is for money; who wish to get rich first, and philosophize afterward. It is for those who have, so far, found neither the time, the means, nor the opportunity to go deeply into the study of metaphysics, but who want results and who are willing to take the conclusions of science as a basis for action, without going into all the processes by which those conclusions were reached.

It is expected that the reader will take the fundamental statements upon faith, just as he would take statements concerning a law of electrical action if they were promulgated by a Marconi or an Edison; and, taking the statements upon faith, that he will prove their truth by acting upon them without fear or hesitation. Every man or woman who does this will certainly get rich; for the science herein applied is an exact science, and failure is impossible. For the benefit, however, of those who wish to investigate philosophical theories and so secure a logical basis for faith, I will here cite certain authorities.

The monistic theory of the universe the theory that One is All, and that All is One; That one Substance manifests itself as the seeming many elements of the material world—is of Hindu origin, and has been gradually winning its way into the thought of the western world for two hundred years. It is the foundation of all the Oriental philosophies, and of those of Descartes, Spinoza, Leibnitz, Schopenhauer, Hegel, and Emerson.

The reader who would dig to the philosophical foundations of this is advised to read Hegel and Emerson for himself. In writing this book I have sacrificed all other considerations to plainness and simplicity of style, so that all might understand. The plan of action laid down herein was deduced from the conclusions of philosophy; it has been thoroughly tested, and bears the supreme test of practical experiment; it works. If you wish to know how the conclusions were arrived at, read the writings of the authors mentioned above; and if you wish to reap the fruits of their philosophies in actual practice, read this book and do exactly as it tells you to do.

Wallace D. Wattles

STUDY GUIDE

Preface

1. In the Preface of *The Science of Getting Rich*, Wallace Wattles references Marconi and Edison as individuals who acted upon statements that they believe to be truths without fear or hesitation. He claims that every man or woman that does this will certainly get rich. Do you believe this to be true? If so, why? Where do you see real world evidence of this?

2. The author advises you to research the philosophical foundations of Hegel and Emerson to learn more about the theory that One is All, and that All is One. Take some time to research at least one of these theorists and summarize what you have discovered.

3. In order to reap the benefits of this book, Wattles encourages you to read this book and do exactly as it tells you to do. Are you ready to do so?

4. Make a list of any blocks (e.g. lack of time, fatigue, family commitments, etc.) of which you are currently aware that could get in your way of practicing this book's suggestions.

5. Clearing blocks may be as simple as committing to 30-minutes a day to focus on the remarkable practices described in this book. As you continue to read Wattles book, for each of the blocks you listed in #4, list corresponding tools offered by the book that you could use to remove them.

Chapter 1

The Right To Be Rich

Whatever may be said in praise of poverty, the fact remains that it is not possible to live a really complete or successful life unless one is rich. No man can rise to his greatest possible height in talent or soul development unless he has plenty of money; for to unfold the soul and to develop talent he must have many things to use, and he cannot have these things unless he has money to buy them with.

A man develops in mind, soul, and body by making use of things, and society is so organized that man must have money in order to become the possessor of things; therefore, the basis of all advancement for man must be the science of getting rich.

The object of all life is development; and everything that lives has an inalienable right to all the development it is capable of attaining Man's right to life means his right to have the free and unrestricted use of all the things which may be necessary to his fullest mental, spiritual, and physical unfoldment; or, in other words, his right to be rich. In this book, I shall not speak of riches in a figurative way; to be really rich does not mean to be satisfied or contented with a little. No man ought to be satisfied with a little if he is capable of using and enjoying more. The purpose of Nature is the advancement and unfoldment of life; and every man should have all that can contribute to the power; elegance, beauty, and richness of life; to be content with less is sinful.

The man who owns all he wants for the living of all the life he is capable of living is rich; and no man who has not plenty of money can have all he wants. Life has advanced so far, and become so complex, that even the most ordinary man or woman requires a great amount of wealth in order to live in a manner that even approaches completeness. Every person naturally wants to become all that they are capable of becoming; this desire to realize innate possibilities is inherent in human nature; we cannot help wanting to be all that we can be. Success in life is becoming what you want to be; you can become what you want to be only by making use of things, and you can have the free use of things only as you become rich enough to buy them. To understand the science of getting rich is therefore the most essential of all knowledge.

There is nothing wrong in wanting to get rich. The desire for riches is really the desire for a richer, fuller, and more abundant life; and that desire is praise worthy. The man who does not desire to live more abundantly is abnormal, and so the man who does not desire to have money enough to buy all he wants is abnormal.

There are three motives for which we live; we live for the body, we live for the mind, we live for the soul. No one of these is better or holier than the other; all are alike desirable, and no one of the three—body, mind, or soul—can live fully if either of the others is cut short of full life and expression. It is not right or noble to live only for the soul and deny mind or body; and it is wrong to live for the intellect and deny body or soul.

We are all acquainted with the loathsome consequences of living for the body and denying both mind and soul; and we see that real life means the complete expression of all that man can give forth through body, mind, and soul. Whatever he can say, no man can be really happy or satisfied unless his body is living fully in every function, and unless the same is true of his mind and his soul. Wherever there is unexpressed possibility, or function not performed, there is unsatisfied desire. Desire is possibility seeking expression, or function seeking performance.

Man cannot live fully in body without good food, comfortable clothing, and warm shelter; and without freedom from excessive toil. Rest and recreation are also necessary to his physical life.

He cannot live fully in mind without books and time to study them, without opportunity for travel and observation, or without intellectual companionship.

To live fully in mind he must have intellectual recreations, and must surround himself with all the objects of art and beauty he is capable of using and appreciating. To live fully in soul, man must have love; and love is denied expression by poverty.

A man's highest happiness is found in the bestowal of benefits on those he loves; love finds its most natural and spontaneous expression in giving. The man who has nothing to give cannot fill his place as a husband or father, as a citizen, or as a man. It is in the use of material things that a man finds full life for his body, develops his mind, and unfolds his soul. It is therefore of supreme importance to him that he should be rich.

It is perfectly right that you should desire to be rich; if you are a normal man or woman you cannot help doing so. It is perfectly right that you should give your best attention to the Science of Getting Rich, for it is the noblest and most necessary of all studies. If you neglect this study, you are derelict in your duty to yourself, to God and humanity; for you can render to God and humanity no greater service than to make the most of yourself.

The Right to Be Rich

1. Wattles opens this book with the declaration, ". . . it is not possible to live a really complete or successful life unless one is rich." Do you believe this statement to be true? Why or why not?

2. If you believe this statement to be true, list three examples of individuals who have wealth and live a "really complete or successful life."

3. He continues by saying that ". . . to unfold the soul and to develop talent he (man) must have many things to use, and he cannot have these things unless he has money to buy them with." Using the three examples that you listed above, provide specific details on the "things to use" that would enable one to "rise to his greatest possible height?"

4. According to Wattles, man's right to life includes his right to be rich. Do you believe you have a right to be rich, simply by being on this earth, or do you believe you have to "do" something to attain wealth? Explain.

5. If you believe that you have to "do" something to get rich, look into your past. Where did you learn this belief? Family? Culture? Religion?

6. Wattles states that "No man ought to be satisfied with a little if he is capable of using and enjoying more." Make a

list of everything you would enjoy having or doing in your life. (E.g. larger house, loving partner, travel, leisure time, etc.)

7. Wattles also states, ". . . to be content with less is sinful." Expand on this concept in your own words.

8. Wattles emphasizes that the desire to become all that we are capable of is inherent in human nature. How does this desire manifest in your life?

9. How have you felt when you have not experienced all that you are capable of?

10. Wattles states that, "Success in life is becoming what you want to be." List the ways in which you are becoming what you want to be.

11. List the ways in which you are not what you want to be.

12. According to this book, not having a desire for money is abnormal and having the desire for riches is actually the praiseworthy desire for a richer, fuller, and more abundant life. Is there any part of you that judges your desire to get rich? If so, why do you believe that you have such a judgment?

13. We live for the equal enrichment of our minds, bodies and souls. Denying any is wrong. Do you give equal weight to the care of your body, mind and soul's needs? If not, for which of the three do you take most care? Why?

14. Desire is "possibility seeking expression" or "function seeking performance". List something that you desire in your life, noting how it fits into this definition of "desire".

15. Rest and recreation are necessary to your physical life. How many hours each week do you dedicate to getting

adequate rest? Similarly, how much time do you dedicate to recreation each week?

16. Noting the hours that you listed for rest and recreation, what would be the ideal hours that you would dedicate to each on a weekly basis?

17. Travel, observation, and intellectual companionship help us live full lives. Do you travel as much as you would wish? If not, describe the type, duration, and frequency of travel that you desire.

18. Do you spend optimal time on reading and studying? If not, how many hours do you currently dedicate to it, and how many hours would you ideally like to dedicate to it?

19. To live fully in your mind, you must surround yourself with all the objects of art and beauty that you are capable of using and appreciating. Have you done so? If not, what more would you want to add to your surroundings?

20. To live fully in your soul is to love. According to Wattles, love is denied expression by poverty. In other words, love cannot flourish in poverty and lack. Write about an example of this lack that you have observed.

21. Love finds its most natural and spontaneous expression in giving. How has love been expressed in your life? How would you desire it to be fully expressed?

22. According to the author, The Science of Getting Rich is the noblest and most necessary of all studies; without which you are derelict in your duty to yourself, to God and humanity. This really shifts most people's perception of this pursuit. When considering that attaining wealth is your obligation to God and to humanity as a whole, how do any feelings of guilt or unworthiness shift for you?

Chapter 2

There Is A Science Of Getting Rich

There is a Science of getting rich, and it is an exact science, like algebra or arithmetic. There are certain laws which govern the process of acquiring riches; once these laws are learned and obeyed by any man, he will get rich with mathematical certainty.

The ownership of money and property comes as a result of doing things in a certain way; those who do things in this Certain Way, whether on purpose or accidentally, get rich; while those who do not do things in this Certain Way, no matter how hard they work or how able they are, remain poor. It is a natural law that like causes always produce like effects; and, therefore, any man or woman who learns to do things in this certain way will infallibly get rich.

That the above statement is true is shown by the following facts: Getting rich is not a matter of environment, for, if it were, all the people in certain neighborhoods would become wealthy; the people of one city would all be rich, while those of other towns would all be poor; or the inhabitants of one state would roll in wealth, while those of an adjoining state would be in poverty.

But everywhere we see rich and poor living side by side, in the same environment, and often engaged in the same vocations. When two men are in the same locality, and in the same business, and one gets rich while the other remains poor, it shows that getting rich is not, primarily, a matter of environment. Some environments may be more favorable than others, but when two men in the same business are in the same neighborhood, and one gets rich while the other fails, it indicates that getting rich is the result of doing things in a Certain Way.

And further, the ability to do things in this certain way is not due solely to the possession of talent, for many people who have great talent remain poor, while other who have very little talent get rich.

Studying the people who have got rich, we find that they are an average lot in all respects, having no greater talents and abilities than other men. It is evident that they do not get rich because they possess talents and abilities that other men have not, but because they happen to do things in a Certain Way.

Getting rich is not the result of saving, or "thrift"; many very penurious people are poor, while free spenders often get rich. Nor is getting rich due to doing things which others fail to do; for two men in the same business often do almost exactly the same things, and one gets rich while the other remains poor or becomes bankrupt. From all these things, we must come to the conclusion that getting rich is the result of doing things in a Certain Way.

If getting rich is the result of doing things in a Certain Way, and if like causes always produce like effects, then any man or woman who can do things in that way can become rich, and the whole matter is brought within the domain of exact science.

The question arises here, whether this Certain Way may not be so difficult that only a few may follow it. This cannot be true, as we have seen, so far as natural ability is concerned. Talented people get rich, and blockheads get rich; intellectually brilliant people get rich, and very stupid people get rich; physically strong people get rich, and weak and sickly people get rich.

Some degree of ability to think and understand is, of course, essential; but in so far natural ability is concerned, any man or woman who has sense enough to read and understand these words can certainly get rich. Also, we have seen that it is not a matter of environment. Location counts for something; one would not go to the heart of the Sahara and expect to do successful business.

Getting rich involves the necessity of dealing with men, and of being where there are people to deal with; and if these people are inclined to deal in the way you want to deal, so much the better. But that is about as far as environment goes.

If anybody else in your town can get rich, so can you; and if anybody else in your state can get rich, so can you. Again, it is not a matter of choosing some particular business or profession. People get rich in every business, and in every profession; while their next door neighbors in the same vocation remain in poverty. It is true that you will do best in a business which you like, and which is congenial to you; and if you have certain talents which are well developed, you will do best in a business which calls for the exercise of those talents. Also, you will do best in a business which is suited to your locality; an ice-cream parlor would do better in a warm climate than in Greenland, and a salmon fishery will succeed better in the Northwest than in Florida, where there are no salmon.

But, aside from these general limitations, getting rich is not dependent upon your engaging in some particular business, but upon your learning to do things in a Certain Way. If you are now in business, and anybody else in your locality is getting rich in the same business, while you are not getting rich, it is because you are not doing things in the same Way that the other person is doing them.

No one is prevented from getting rich by lack of capital. True, as you get capital the increase becomes more easy and rapid; but one who has capital is already rich, and does not need to consider how to become so. No matter how poor you may be, if you begin to do things in the Certain Way you will begin to get rich; and you will begin to have capital. The getting of capital is a part of the process of getting rich; and it is a part of the result which invariably follows the doing of things in the Certain Way. You may be the poorest man on the continent, and be deeply in debt; you may have neither friends, influence, nor resources; but if you begin to do things in this way, you must infallibly begin to get rich, for like causes must produce like effects. If you have no capital, you can get capital; if you are in the wrong business, you can get into the right business; if you are in the wrong location, you can go to the right location; and you can do so by beginning in your present business and in your present location to do things in the Certain Way which causes success.

STUDY GUIDE

There Is a Science of Getting Rich

1. Like arithmetic, there is an exact science to getting rich. According to Wattles, once the laws are learned and practiced, you will get rich with mathematical certainty. How does this absolute statement make you feel?

2. It is a natural law that "like causes always produce like effects". Such is the case with acquiring wealth. Can you provide an example of how "like causes produce like effects"?

3. Wealth is not determined by environment, talent, saving, or doing the things that others fail to do. Similarly, all types of people get rich. This all leads to the tenet that gaining wealth is the result of doing things in a Certain Way. Do you carry any old beliefs that environment, talent, saving or doing things that others fail to do create wealth? If so, seek out an example of someone who created wealth without the use of any of these determinants.

4. Attaining wealth is not reliant upon choosing some particular business or profession, as there are rich and poor in all. However it is true that you will do best in a business that you like, one that also uses your talents. Do you currently have a business idea in mind that you like, one that uses your talents? If so, describe it. If not, have faith and remain open to discovering it. Signs and suggestions will

come to you because you are reading this book and have committed to attaining wealth in your life.

5. If you don't have capital to support your business, rest assured that it will come to you as you do things in a Certain Way. Wattles encourages you to begin in your present business in your present location, emphasizing that doing things in the Certain Way will cause success. Describe your current business and its present location. If you don't have a current business, describe the business that you would like to start.

Chapter 3

Is Opportunity Monopolized?

No man is kept poor because opportunity has been taken away from him; because other people have monopolized the wealth, and have put a fence around it. You may be shut off from engaging in business in certain lines, but there are other channels open to you. Probably it would be hard for you to get control of any of the great railroad systems; that field is pretty well monopolized. But the electric railway business is still in its infancy, and offers plenty of scope for enterprise; and it will be but a very few years until traffic and transportation through the air will become a great industry, and in all its branches will give employment to hundreds of thousands, and perhaps to millions, of people. Why not turn your attention to the development of aerial transportation, instead of competing with J.J. Hill and others for a chance in the steam railway world?

It is quite true that if you are a workman in the employ of the steel trust you have very little chance of becoming the owner of the plant in which you work; but it is also true that if you will commence to act in a Certain Way, you can soon leave the employ of the steel trust; you can buy a farm of from ten to forty acres, and engage in business as a producer of foodstuffs. There is great opportunity at this time for men who will live upon small tracts of land and cultivate the same intensively; such men will certainly get rich. You may say that it is impossible for you to get the land, but I am going to prove to you that it is not impossible, and that you can certainly get a farm if you will go to work in a Certain Way.

At different periods the tide of opportunity sets in different directions, according to the needs of the whole, and the particular stage of social evolution which has been reached. At present, in America, it is setting toward agriculture and the allied industries and professions. To-day, opportunity is open before the factory worker in his line. It is open before the business man who supplies the farmer more than before the one who supplies the factory worker; and before the professional man who waits upon the farmer more than before the one who serves the working class. There is abundance of opportunity for the man who will go with the tide, instead of trying to swim against it.

So the factory workers, either as individuals or as a class, are not deprived of opportunity. The workers are not being "kept down" by their masters; they are not being "ground" by the trusts and combinations of capital. As a class, they are where they are because they do not do things in a Certain Way. If the workers of America chose to do so, they could follow the example of their brothers in Belgium and other countries, and establish great department stores and co-operative industries; they could elect men of their own class to office, and pass laws favoring the development of such cooperative industries; and in a few years they could take peaceable possession of the industrial field.

The working class may become the master class whenever they will begin to do things in a Certain Way; the law of wealth is the same for them as it is for all others. This they must learn; and they will remain where they are as long as they continue to do as they do. The individual worker, however, is not held down by the ignorance or the mental slothfulness of his class; he can follow the tide of opportunity to riches, and this book will tell him how. No one is kept in poverty by a shortness in the supply of riches; there is more than enough for all. A palace as large as the capitol at Washington might be built for every family on earth from the building material in the United States alone; and under intensive cultivation, this country would produce wool, cotton, linen, and silk enough to cloth each person in the world finer than Solomon was arrayed in all his glory; together with food enough to feed them all luxuriously.

The visible supply is practically inexhaustible; and the invisible supply really IS inexhaustible. Everything you see on earth is made from one original substance, out of which all things proceed. New Forms are constantly being made, and older ones are dissolving; but all are shapes assumed by One Thing. There is no limit to the supply of Formless Stuff, or Original Substance. The universe is made out of it; but it was not all used in making the universe. The spaces in, through, and between the forms of the visible universe are permeated and filled with the Original Substance; with the formless Stuff; with the raw material of all things. Ten thousand times as much as has been made might still be made, and even then we should not have exhausted the supply of universal raw material.

No man, therefore, is poor because nature is poor, or because there is not enough to go around. Nature is an inexhaustible storehouse of riches; the supply will never run short. Original Substance is alive with creative energy, and is constantly producing more forms. When the supply of building material is exhausted, more will be produced; when the soil is exhausted so that food stuffs and materials for clothing will no longer grow upon it, it will be renewed or more soil will be made. When all the gold and silver has been dug from the earth, if man is still in such a stage of social development that he needs gold and silver, more will produced from the Formless. The Formless Stuff responds to the needs of man; it will not let him be without any good thing. This is true of man collectively; the race as a whole is always abundantly rich, and if individuals are poor, it is because they do not follow the Certain Way of doing things which makes the individual man rich. The Formless Stuff is intelligent; it is stuff which thinks. It is alive, and is always impelled toward more life.

It is the natural and inherent impulse of life to seek to live more; it is the nature of intelligence to enlarge itself, and of consciousness to seek to extend its boundaries and find fuller expression. The universe of forms has been made by Formless Living Substance, throwing itself into form in order to express itself more fully.

The universe is a great Living Presence, always moving inherently toward more life and fuller functioning. Nature is formed for the advancement of life; its impelling motive is the increase of life. For this cause, everything which can possibly minister to life is bountifully provided; there can be no lack unless God is to contradict himself and nullify his own works.

You are not kept poor by lack in the supply of riches; it is a fact which I shall demonstrate a little farther on that even the resources of the Formless Supply are at the command of the man or woman will act and think in a Certain Way.

STUDY GUIDE

Is Opportunity Monopolized?

1. An indication of the timelessness of Wallace Wattles' teachings is revealed in the first paragraph of this chapter, when he encourages his readers to pursue the "new" enterprise of air travel. He certainly was right in his predictions about the business opportunities that air travel has offered. How many other opportunities can you think of that weren't even around ten years ago?

2. Wattles emphasizes that if you work in a Certain Way, then you can leave your nine-to-five job, buy land and create greater success. While farming may not provide the financial opportunities that it did during the author's time, owning land has always been a wise investment. Have you ever had a desire to own land? If so, describe what you would like in as much detail as possible.

3. Whether you have considered purchasing land as an investment or not, take a moment to image owning some. Where, geographically would the land be located? You may wish to own several parcels of land in various countries. Allow your imagination to flourish.

4. What would you do with the land? Keep it? Put commercial or residential real estate on it? Cultivate it? Build a nature preserve on it? Build a theme park on it? Live on it?

5. "There is abundance of opportunity for the man who will go with the tide, instead of trying to swim against it." What

do you consider to be the tide of the future? How might you take advantage of the current trends in the world?

6. Wattles talks of becoming a part of "co-operative" industries. What would you consider to be present-day co-operative industries?

7. Responsible, green-sensitive business is becoming very popular. How might you benefit from getting more involved in this industry?

8. How might your business ideas be incorporated into the green movement? Do you think doing so would help or hinder future business?

9. Wattles points out that there is an abundance of resources in the world and that no one is a victim of external lack. "The visible supply is practically inexhaustible; and the invisible supply really IS inexhaustible." Take a moment and contemplate this statement. With the constant barrage of media attention on the "lack" of resources available to us, in what context can Wattles' statement be true?

10. Everything you see on earth is made from one original substance, out of which all things proceed. Do you believe this statement to be true? Please expand upon your understanding of this statement.

11. According to Wattles, "Original substance is alive with creative energy, and it is constantly producing more forms." Provide at least three examples of this in the world.

12. It takes an element of faith to believe that "The Formless Stuff responds to the needs of man; it will not let him be without any good thing." On a scale from one to ten, how much faith do you have in this statement? (1 being, I do

not believe it to be true at all, and 10 being, I absolutely believe it to be true.)

1——2——3——4——5——6——7——8——9——10

13. The Formless Stuff thinks, is alive and is always impelled towards more life. It is the nature of intelligence to enlarge itself. Where do you find examples of this in nature?

14. Do you know of any examples to counter the statement listed in #13? If so, what?

15. According to Wallace Wattles, "There can be no lack unless God is to contradict himself and nullify his own works." Do you believe that God created the world's abundance?

16. If not, how do you account for the abundance that exists in the world?

17. If the resources of the Formless Supply are at the command of the man or woman who would act and think in a Certain Way, then list the ways in which you have you been acting and thinking to date that would countermand the Formless Supply to grow in your favor?

Chapter 4

The First Principle
In The Science Of Getting Rich

Thought is the only power which can produce tangible riches from the Formless Substance. The stuff from which all things are made is a substance which thinks, and a thought of form in this substance produces the form. Original Substance moves according to its thoughts; every form and process you see in nature is the visible expression of a thought in Original Substance. As the Formless Stuff thinks of a form, it takes that form; as it thinks of a motion, it makes that motion. That is the way all things were created. We live in a thought world, which is part of a thought universe. The thought of a moving universe extended throughout Formless Substance, and the Thinking Stuff moving according to that thought, took the form of systems of planets, and maintains that form. Thinking Substance takes the form of its thought, and moves according to the thought. Holding the idea of a circling system of suns and worlds, it takes the form of these bodies, and moves them as it thinks. Thinking the form of a slow-growing oak tree, it moves accordingly, and produces the tree, though centuries may be required to do the work. In creating, the Formless seems to move according to the lines of motion it has established; the thought of an oak tree does not cause the instant formation of a full-grown tree, but it does start in motion the forces which will produce the tree, along established lines of growth. Every thought of form, held in thinking Substance, causes the creation of the form, but always, or at least generally, along lines of growth and action already established.

The thought of a house of a certain construction, if it were impressed upon Formless Substance, might not cause the instant formation, of the house; but it would cause the turning of creative energies already working in trade and commerce into such channels as to result in the speedy building of the house. And if there were no existing channels through which the creative energy could work, then the house would be formed directly from primal substance, without waiting for the slow processes of the organic and inorganic world.

No thought of form can be impressed upon Original Substance without causing the creation of the form. Man is a thinking center, and can originate thought. All the forms that man fashions with his hands must first exist in his thought; he cannot shape a thing until he has thought that thing.

And so far man has confined his efforts wholly to the work of his hands; he has applied manual labor to the world of forms, seeking to change or modify those already existing. He has never thought of trying to cause the creation of new forms by impressing his thoughts upon Formless Substance. When man has a thought-form, he takes material from the forms of nature, and makes an image of the form which is in his mind. He has, so far, made little or no effort to co-operate with Formless Intelligence; to work "with the Father." He has not dreamed that he can "do what he seeth the Father doing." Man reshapes and modifies existing forms by manual labor; he has given no attention to the question whether he may not produce things from Formless Substance by communicating his thoughts to it. We propose to prove that he may do so; to prove that any man or woman may do so, and to show how. As our first step, we must lay down three fundamental propositions.

First, we assert that there is one original formless stuff, or substance, from which all things are made. All the seemingly many elements are but different presentations of one element; all the many forms found in organic and inorganic nature are but different shapes, made from the same stuff. And this stuff is thinking stuff; a thought held in it produces the form of the thought. Thought, in thinking substance, produces shapes. Man is a thinking center, capable of original thought; if man can communicate his thought to original thinking substance, he can cause the creation, or formation, of the thing he thinks about. To summarize this—There is a thinking stuff from which all things are made, and which, in its original state, permeates, penetrates, and fills the interspaces of the universe. A thought, in this substance, Produces the thing that is imaged by the thought.

Man can form things in his thought, and, by impressing his thought upon formless substance, can cause the thing he thinks about to be created. It may be asked if I can prove these statements; and without going into details, I answer that I can do so, both by logic and experience. Reasoning back from the phenomena of form and thought, I come to one original thinking substance; and reasoning forward from this thinking substance, I come to man's power to cause the formation of the thing he thinks about.

And by experiment, I find the reasoning true; and this is my strongest proof. If one man who reads this book gets rich by doing what it tells him to do, that is evidence in support of my claim; but if every man who does what it tells him to do gets rich, that is positive proof until some one goes through the process and fails. The theory is true until the process fails; and this process will not fail, for every man who does exactly what this book tells him to do will get rich.

I have said that men get rich by doing things in a Certain Way; and in order to do so, men must become able to think in a certain way. A man's way of doing things is the direct result of the way he thinks about things.

To do things in a way you want to do them, you will have to acquire the ability to think the way you want to think; this is the first step toward getting rich. To think what you want to think is to think TRUTH, regardless of appearances.

Every man has the natural and inherent power to think what he wants to think, but it requires far more effort to do so than it does to think the thoughts which are suggested by appearances. To think according to appearance is easy; to think truth regardless of appearances is laborious, and requires the expenditure of more power than any other work man is called upon to perform.

There is no labor from which most people shrink as they do from that of sustained and consecutive thought; it is the hardest work in the world. This is especially true when truth is contrary to appearances. Every appearance in the visible world tends to produce a corresponding form in the mind which observes it; and this can only be prevented by holding the thought of the TRUTH.

To look upon the appearance of disease will produce the form of disease in your own mind, and ultimately in your body, unless you hold the thought of the truth, which is that there is no disease; it is only an appearance, and the reality is health.

To look upon the appearances of poverty will produce corresponding forms in your own mind, unless you hold to the truth that there is no poverty; there is only abundance. To think health when surrounded by the appearances of disease, or to think riches when in the midst of appearances of poverty, requires power; but he who acquires this power becomes a MASTER MIND. He can conquer fate; he can have what he wants.

This power can only be acquired by getting hold of the basic fact which is behind all appearances; and that fact is that there is one Thinking Substance, from which and by which all things are made. Then we must grasp the truth that every thought held in this substance becomes a form, and that man can so impress his thoughts upon it as to cause them to take form and become visible things. When we realize this, we lose all doubt and fear, for we know that we can create what we want to create; we can get what we want to have, and can become what we want to be. As a first step toward getting rich, you must believe the three fundamental statements given previously in this chapter; and in order to emphasize them. I repeat them here: There is a thinking stuff from which all things are made, and which, in its original state, permeates, penetrates, and fills the interspaces of the universe.

A thought, in this substance, Produces the thing that is imaged by the thought. Man can form things in his thought, and, by impressing his thought upon formless substance, can cause the thing he thinks about to be created. You must lay aside all other concepts of the universe than this monistic one; and you must dwell upon this until it is fixed in your mind, and has become your habitual thought. Read these creed statements over and over again; fix every word upon your memory, and meditate upon them until you firmly believe what they say. If a doubt comes to you, cast it aside as a sin. Do not listen to arguments against this idea; do not go to churches or lectures where a contrary concept of things is taught or preached. Do not read magazines or books which teach a different idea; if you get mixed up in your faith, all your efforts will be in vain.

Do not ask why these things are true, nor speculate as to how they can be true; simply take them on trust. The science of getting rich begins with the absolute acceptance of this faith.

STUDY GUIDE

*The First Principle
In the Science of Getting Rich*

1. If thought is the only power that can produce tangible riches from the Formless Substance, then take some time to focus on your thoughts around abundance. For 24 hours, carry a small notebook around with you and make notes on any thoughts that you have about money.

2. Do you note any patterns in your thoughts around abundance? Do you perhaps think, "Yes, someday I'll be rich" and project success somewhere into the future? If so, how might this belief be serving you at this time?

3. "Every form and process you see in nature is the visual expression of a thought in Original Substance." Take this testament and apply it to three real-life examples in nature. For example, a raindrop that is falling from the top of a leaf to the bottom is a visual expression of a thought in Original Substance. Then take a moment to reflect upon this realization.

   Example 1: _____

   Example 2: _____

   Example 3: _____

4. If every thought form causes the creation of that form, then how have your thoughts caused the creation of things in your life? List one positive experience that you have had, along with one negative. What thought forms do you believe created those experiences?

5. "Man cannot shape a thing until he has thought that thing." Reflect on your life experiences. Try to note a time when you thought you "spontaneously" shaped something in your life. Reconsider. Had you "thought" about that experience at some point in your existence? Please describe your findings.

6. There are three fundamental propositions:
   1. There is one original stuff, or substance, from which all things are made.
   2. A thought, in this substance, produces the thing that is imagined by the thought.
   3. Man can form things in his thought, and by impressing his thought upon formless substance, can cause the thing he thinks about to be created.

The first step to manifesting what you want in your life is to believe these three propositions. Re-write them in your own words, including an example for each.

7. Wattles suggests that you lay aside all other concepts of the universe and dwell upon these propositions until they are fixed in your mind. Read these statements over and over again, and meditate on them until you firmly believe what they say. Cast any doubt aside and stay away from churches, lectures, books, magazines or anywhere else where a contrary thought is preached. For the next 30 days, repeat each of the propositions aloud first thing in the morning and then last thing at night. After speaking

them aloud, meditate upon them. Note any experiences you have in relation to following this practice.

8. "A man's way of doing things is a direct result of the way he thinks about things." For the duration of the day, reflect upon your thoughts. How are your thoughts manifesting into form throughout your day? Record your thoughts and the corresponding experiences that they bring.

9. "To think what you want to think is to think TRUTH, regardless of appearances." What do you think Wattles means in this statement?

10. Wallace Wattles says that disease is only an appearance and that the reality is health. Looking upon the "appearance of disease" will produce the form of disease in your mind and ultimately in your body. Do you believe this to be true? If not, why not? If so, where do you see evidence of this in the world?

11. There is only abundance. However, if you look upon the appearances of poverty, you will produce corresponding forms in your own mind. Where have you focused on abundance, and how has it manifested in your life?

12. A MASTERMIND is defined as someone who acquires the power to think health and wealth when surrounded by appearances of disease and lack. Do you have what it takes to become a MASTERMIND? Give one example of how you or someone you know has been a MASTERMIND by defying unwanted appearances in your lives.

13. At the end of this chapter, Wallace Wattles encourages you to take the tenets of his teachings on faith, stating, "The science of getting rich begins with the absolute acceptance of this faith". How strong is your faith in the unknown?

14. How strong is your faith in Wattles' teachings? Rate the strength of your belief on a scale from one to ten (one being you have little faith, and ten being you have unwavering faith).

15. What do you need in order to strengthen your faith in your ability to acquire wealth in your life?

Chapter 5

Increasing Life

YOU must get rid of the last vestige of the old idea that there is a Deity whose will it is that you should be poor, or whose purposes may be served by keeping you in poverty.

The Intelligent Substance which is All, and in All, and which lives in All and lives in you, is a consciously Living Substance. Being a consciously living substance, It must have the nature and inherent desire of every living intelligence for increase of life. Every living thing must continually seek for the enlargement of its life, because life, in the mere act of living, must increase itself.

A seed, dropped into the ground, springs into activity, and in the act of living produces a hundred more seeds; life, by living, multiplies itself. It is forever Becoming More; it must do so, if it continues to be at all. Intelligence is under this same necessity for continuous increase. Every thought we think makes it necessary for us to think another thought; consciousness is continually expanding. Every fact we learn leads us to the learning of another fact; knowledge is continually increasing. Every talent we cultivate brings to the mind the desire to cultivate another talent; we are subject to the urge of life, seeking expression, which ever drives us on to know more, to do more, and to be more.

In order to know more, do more, and be more we must have more; we must have things to use, for we learn, and do, and become, only by using things. We must get rich, so that we can live more.

The desire for riches is simply the capacity for larger life seeking fulfillment; every desire is the effort of an unexpressed possibility to come into action. It is power seeking to manifest which causes desire. That which makes you want more money is the same as that which makes the plant grow; it is Life, seeking fuller expression.

The One Living Substance must be subject to this inherent law of all life; it is permeated with the desire to live more; that is why it is under the necessity of creating things. The One Substance desires to live more in you; hence it wants you to have all the things you It is the desire of God that you should get rich. He wants you to get rich because he can express himself better through you if you have plenty of things to use in giving him expression. He can live more in you if you have unlimited command of the means of life. The universe desires you to have everything you want to have.

Nature is friendly to your plans.
Everything is naturally for you.
Make up your mind that this is true.

It is essential, however that your purpose should harmonize with the purpose that is in All. You must want real life, not mere pleasure of sensual gratification. Life is the performance of function; and the individual really lives only when he performs every function, physical, mental, and spiritual, of which he is capable, without excess in any. You do not want to get rich in order to live swinishly, for the gratification of animal desires; that is not life. But the performance of every physical function is a part of life, and no one lives completely who denies the impulses of the body a normal and healthful expression.

You do not want to get rich solely to enjoy mental pleasures, to get knowledge, to gratify ambition, to outshine others, to be famous. All these are a legitimate part of life, but the man who lives for the pleasures of the intellect alone will only have a partial life, and he will never be satisfied with his lot. You do not want to get rich solely for the good of others, to lose yourself for the salvation of mankind, to experience the joys of philanthropy and sacrifice. The joys of the soul are only a part of life; and they are no better or nobler than any other part.

You want to get rich in order that you may eat, drink, and be merry when it is time to do these things; in order that you may surround yourself with beautiful things, see distant lands, feed your mind, and develop your intellect; in order that you may love men and do kind things, and be able to play a good part in helping the world to find truth. But remember that extreme altruism is no better and no nobler than extreme selfishness; both are mistakes. Get rid of the idea that God wants you to sacrifice yourself for others, and that you can secure his favor by doing so; God requires nothing of the kind.

What he wants is that you should make the most of yourself, for yourself, and for others; and you can help others more by making the most of yourself than in any other way. You can make the most of yourself only by getting rich; so it is right and praiseworthy that you should give your first and best thought to the work of acquiring wealth. Remember, however, that the desire of Substance is for all, and its movements must be for more life to all; it cannot be made to work for less life to any, because it is equally in all, seeking riches and life.

Intelligent Substance will make things for you, but it will not take things away from some one else and give them to you. You must get rid of the thought of competition. You are to create, not to compete for what is already created. You do not have to take anything away from any one. You do not have to drive sharp bargains. You do not have to cheat, or to take advantage. You do not need to let any man work for you for less than he earns.

You do not have to covet the property of others, or to look at it with wishful eyes; no man has anything of which you cannot have the like, and that without taking what he has away from him. You are to become a creator, not a competitor; you are going to get what you want, but in such a way that when you get it every other man will have more than he has now. I am aware that there are men who get a vast amount of money by proceeding in direct opposition to the statements in the paragraph above, and may add a word of explanation here. Men of the plutocratic type, who become very rich, do so sometimes purely by their extraordinary ability on the plane of competition; and sometimes they unconsciously relate themselves to Substance in its great purposes and movements for the general racial upbuilding through industrial evolution. Rockefeller, Carnegie, Morgan, et al., have been the unconscious agents of the Supreme in the necessary work of systematizing and organizing productive industry; and in the end, their work will contribute immensely toward increased life for all. Their day is nearly over; they have organized production, and will soon be succeeded by the agents of the multitude, who will organize the machinery of distribution.

The multi-millionaires are like the monster reptiles of the prehistoric eras; they play a necessary part in the evolutionary process, but the same Power which produced them will dispose of them. And it is well to bear in mind that they have never been really rich; a record of the private lives of most of this class will show that they have really been the most abject and wretched of the poor. Riches secured on the competitive plane are never satisfactory and permanent; they are yours to-day, and another's tomorrow.

Remember, if you are to become rich in a scientific and certain way, you must rise entirely out of the competitive thought. You must never think for a moment that the supply is limited. Just as soon as you begin to think that all the money is being "cornered" and controlled by bankers and others, and that you must exert yourself to get laws passed to stop this process, and so on; in that moment you drop into the competitive mind, and your power to cause creation is gone for the time being; and what is worse, you will probably arrest the creative movements you have already instituted.

KNOW that there are countless millions of dollars' worth of gold in the mountains of the earth, not yet brought to light; and know that if there were not, more would be created from Thinking Substance to supply your needs. KNOW that the money you need will come, even if it is necessary for a thousand men to be led to the discovery of new gold mines tomorrow. Never look at the visible supply; look always at the limitless riches in Formless Substance, and KNOW that they are coming to you as fast as you can receive and use them. Nobody, by cornering the visible supply, can prevent you from getting what is yours.

So never allow yourself to think for an instant that all the best building spots will be taken before you get ready to build your house, unless you hurry. Never worry about the trusts and combines, and get anxious for fear they will soon come to own the whole earth. Never get afraid that you will lose what you want because some other person "beats you to it." That cannot possibly happen; you are not seeking any thing that is possessed by anybody else; you are causing what you want to be created from formless Substance, and the supply is without limits. Stick to the formulated statement: There is a thinking stuff from which all things are made, and which, in its original state, permeates, penetrates, and fills the inter-spaces of the universe. A thought, in this substance, produces the thing that is imaged by the thought. Man can form things in his thought, and, by impressing his thought upon formless substance, can cause the thing he thinks about to be created.

STUDY GUIDE

Increasing Life

1. Wattles opens this chapter with the statement, "You must get rid of the last vestige of the old idea that there is a Deity whose will it is that you should be poor, or whose purposes may be served by keeping you in poverty." Make a list of old "lack" ideas that you still need to work through.

2. Power seeking to manifest, causes desire. According to Wattles, "That which makes you want money is the same as that which makes the plant grow; it is Life, seeking fuller expression." How do you feel about wanting to gain more wealth when he frames your desire in this way? In other words, if your desire for wealth is as natural as a plant that seeks growth, where does any guilt you might have about greed fit into the equation?

3. Take some time to do a creative endeavor. Draw a picture, or find a photo of a plant or tree that is naturally and wonderfully growing. Beside that picture or photo, draw or construct in some way a representation of you and your desire for money in a way that parallels the plant's natural growing process. At the bottom of your rendering, write the quote, "That which makes me want money is the same as that which makes the plant grow; it is my Life, seeking fuller expression. I welcome financial growth in my life." Put this rendering somewhere in your home or office where you can view it often. Reflect upon this notion, and be open to the freedom that it creates within you.

4. Wallace states, "The One Substance desires to live more in you." If the One Substance is creation or that which created this world, then make a list of all the ways in which it can express itself more in your life.

5. The universe desires you to have everything you want to have. Nature is friendly to your plans.

   Nature is friendly to your plans.
   Everything is naturally for you.
   Make up your mind that this is true.

Reflect on the above phrases for 15 minutes. In your deepest self, do you believe them to be true? Do you believe that there is a benevolent force that supports you in manifesting your desires? If there is any doubt, go inside and explore it. What does it fear? What does it need from you so that it can be transformed?

6. Wallace warns that greed and excess is not in balance with the purpose of All. He states that, "The man who lives for the pleasures of the intellect alone will only have a partial life . . ." He also warns you about getting rich solely for the good of others. Contemplate your desire for wealth. Is your reason for this desire one in which you wish to live fully and unbind yourself from your limited thoughts, or is it rooted in your desire to overindulge?

7. Make a list of the things you would like to experience, have, or give once you've attained your desired wealth.

8. Review the list you just created. Put an (×) beside anything that, in reflection, you would consider to be "excessive." Go through the list again, and put a (✓) beside anything you consider altruistic or in balance with the purpose of All.

9. What did you learn about yourself in creating and reviewing your list? Do you believe you have a good balance of gratification and altruism?

10. Wallace encourages you to get rid of the idea that God wants you to sacrifice yourself, stating that God requires nothing of the kind. Is there a part of you that is still caught in the apparent nobility of sacrifice? Reflect upon your current lifestyle. Where are you sacrificing in your life? Write a list of how and what you are sacrificing. It might be in recreation time, in giving up your desires to please your family and friends, taking less pay than you believe you deserve, etc.

11. Wallace states that, "You can help others more by making the most of yourself than in any other way." Imagine a life in which all of your desires are manifest. How do you see yourself helping others while living your dreams? Write about what you experience in your mind's eye, with as much detail as possible.

12. "Intelligent Substance will make things for you, but it will not take things away from someone else and give them to you." You must rid yourself of the idea of competition— when you win, someone else loses. "You are to become a creator, not a competitor." How do you maintain a sense of competitiveness in your life? Make a list of the ways in which you see yourself in competition. When do you experience envy or jealousy in your life? Most likely when you are experiencing these feelings, you are caught in a web of competitiveness.

13. Wattles emphasizes that the multi-millionaires of his era have never been really rich. Records of their private lives revealed that they lived lives of poverty. This clearly does not mean that they were financially poverty-stricken, but poor in other ways. In what ways do you think they may have been poor?

14. Take some time to investigate Rockefeller, Carnegie or Morgan. How did they suffer in their lives? What were their personal lives lacking that money could not buy?

15. The author cautions never to think for a moment that supply is limited. Doing so will halt the flow of abundance to you and could "arrest the creative movements you have already instituted." Consider a time when you really felt great fear and lack around attracting abundance into your life. Briefly describe the energy that you created and fixated upon. What were the results of that energy?

16. "Never look at the visible supply; look always at the limitless riches in Formless Substance, and KNOW that they are coming to you as fast as you can receive and use them." Allow yourself to imagine this scenario for as long as you can. When you have lost the image of abundance coming your way, what thought arose in your mind? In other words, what thoughts pulled you from your image of great abundance? Write about it, and the belief that might have stopped you.

17. At the end of this chapter, the author asserts that you should never worry, nor get afraid or anxious. For the next week, make a conscious effort to catch yourself when you start to feel anxiety around abundance. When you do, say this phrase to yourself three times, "Man can form things in his thought, and, by impressing his thought upon formless substance, can cause the thing he thinks about to be created," then take a couple of minutes and visualize a life full of abundance for yourself in as much detail as possible. Shift your thoughts, and change your energy.

Chapter 6

How Riches Come To You

When I say that you do not have to drive sharp bargains, I do not mean that you do not have to drive any bargains at all, or that you are above the necessity for having any dealings with your fellow men. I mean that you will not need to deal with them unfairly; you do not have to get something for nothing, but can give to every man more than you take from him. You cannot give every man more in cash market value than you take from him, but you can give him more in use value than the cash value of the thing you take from him. The paper, ink, and other material in this book may not be worth the money you pay for it; but if the ideas suggested by it bring you thousands of dollars, you have not been wronged by those who sold it to you; they have given you a great use value for a small cash value.

Let us suppose that I own a picture by one of the great artists, which, in any civilized community, is worth thousands of dollars. I take it to Baffin Ray, and by "salesmanship" induce an Eskimo to give a bundle of furs worth $500 for it. I have really wronged him, for he has no use for the picture; it has no use value to him; it will not add to his life.

But suppose I give him a gun worth $50 for his furs; then he has made a good bargain. He has use for the gun; it will get him many more furs and much food; it will add to his life in every way; it will make him rich. When you rise from the competitive to the creative plane, you can scan your business transactions very strictly, and if you are selling any man anything which does not add more to his life than the thing he give you in exchange, you can afford to stop it. You do not have to beat anybody in business. And if you are in a business which does beat people, get out of it at once.

Give every man more in use value than you take from him in cash value; then you are adding to the life of the world by every business transaction. If you have people working for you, you must take from them more in cash value than you pay them in wages; but you can so organize your business that it will be filled with the principle of advancement, and so that each employee who wishes to do so may advance a little every day.

You can make your business do for your employees what this book is doing for you. You can so conduct your business that it will be a sort of ladder, by which every employee who will take the trouble may climb to riches himself; and given the opportunity, if he will not do so it is not your fault. And finally, because you are to cause the creation of your riches from Formless Substance which permeates all your environment, it does not follow that they are to take shape from the atmosphere and come into being before your eyes.

If you want a sewing machine, for instance, I do not mean to tell you that you are to impress the thought of a sewing machine on Thinking Substance until the machine is formed without hands, in the room where you sit, or elsewhere. But if you want a sewing machine, hold the mental image of it with the most positive certainty that it is being made, or is on its way to you. After once forming the thought, have the most absolute and unquestioning faith that the sewing machine is coming; never think of it, or speak, of it, in any other way than as being sure to arrive. Claim it as already yours.

It will be brought to you by the power of the Supreme Intelligence, acting upon the minds of men. If you live in Maine, it may be that a man will be brought from Texas or Japan to engage in some transaction which will result in your getting what you want. If so, the whole matter will be as much to that man's advantage as it is to yours.

Do not forget for a moment that the Thinking Substance is through all, in all, communicating with all, and can influence all. The desire of Thinking Substance for fuller life and better living has caused the creation of all the sewing machines already made; and it can cause the creation of millions more, and will, whenever men set it in motion by desire and faith, and by acting in a Certain Way. You can certainly have a sewing machine in your house; and it is just as certain that you can have any other thing or things which you want, and which you will use for the advancement of your own life and the lives of others. You need not hesitate about asking largely; "it is your Father's pleasure to give you the kingdom," said Jesus.

Original Substance wants to live all that is possible in you, and wants you to have all that you can or will use for the living of the most abundant life. If you fix upon your consciousness the fact that the desire you feel for the possession of riches is one with the desire of Omnipotence for more complete expression, your faith becomes invincible. Once I saw a little boy sitting at a piano, and vainly trying to bring harmony out of the keys; and I saw that he was grieved and provoked by his inability to play real music. I asked him the cause of his vexation, and he answered, "I can feel the music in me, but I can't make my hands go right." The music in him was the URGE of Original Substance, containing all the possibilities of all life; all that there is of music was seeking expression through the child.

God, the One Substance, is trying to live and do and enjoy things through humanity. He is saying "I want hands to build wonderful structures, to play divine harmonies, to paint glorious pictures; I want feet to run my errands, eyes to see my beauties, tongues to tell mighty truths and to sing marvelous songs," and so on. All that there is of possibility is seeking expression through men. God wants those who can play music to have pianos and every other instrument, and to have the means to cultivate their talents to the fullest extent; He wants those who can appreciate beauty to be able to surround themselves with beautiful things; He wants those who can discern truth to have every opportunity to travel and observe; He wants those who can appreciate dress to be beautifully clothed, and those who can appreciate good food to be luxuriously fed.

He wants all these things because it is Himself that enjoys and appreciates them; it is God who wants to play, and sing, and enjoy beauty, and proclaim truth and wear fine clothes, and eat good foods. "It is God that worketh in you to will and to do," said Paul.

The desire you feel for riches is the infinite, seeking to express Himself in you as He sought to find expression in the little boy at the piano. So you need not hesitate to ask largely. Your part is to focalize and express the desire to God. This is a difficult point with most people; they retain something of the old idea that poverty and self-sacrifice are pleasing to God. They look upon poverty as a part of the plan, a necessity of nature. They have the idea that God has finished His work, and made all that He can make, and that the majority of men must stay poor because there is not enough to go around. They hold to so much of this erroneous thought that they feel ashamed to ask for wealth; they try not to want more than a very modest competence, just enough to make them fairly comfortable.

I recall now the case of one student who was told that he must get in mind a clear picture of the things he desired, so that the creative thought of them might be impressed on Formless Substance. He was a very poor man, living in a rented house, and having only what he earned from day to day; and he could not grasp the fact that all wealth was his. So, after thinking the matter over, he decided that he might reasonably ask for a new rug for the floor of his best room, and an anthracite coal stove to heat the house during the cold weather. Following the instructions given in this book, he obtained these things in a few months; and then it dawned upon him that he had not asked enough. He went through the house in which he lived, and planned all the improvements he would like to make in it; he mentally added a bay window here and a room there, until it was complete in his mind as his ideal home; and then he planned its furnishings.

Holding the whole picture in his mind, he began living in the Certain Way, and moving toward what he wanted; and he owns the house now, and is rebuilding it after the form of his mental image. And now, with still larger faith, he is going on to get greater things. It has been unto him according to his faith, and it is so with you and with all of us.

How Riches Come to You

1. Wallace Wattles opens this chapter with the statement, "You will not need to deal with (fellow men) unfairly; you do not have to get something for nothing, but can give to every man more than you take from him." He goes on to say that the giving does not have to be in cash value, and can be in energetic value. Reflect on your life, and find at least three times that you gave more back to someone than you received. Write these scenarios down.

2. How did you feel in each of the scenarios above? Did you feel good about yourself? Were you feeling overburdened or fatigued by the giving?

3. You need to be sure that when giving, you do not burn yourself out energetically. Think of a situation where you felt exhausted after giving. Look deep into your heart and ask yourself why you gave. Was the underlying motive that you felt unworthy of love and over-gave of yourself in order to be accepted? Write about the experience and your motivations behind it.

4. Each time you find yourself overtaxed, stop and examine why. If you are giving beyond your energetic threshold and are fatigued, do not give so much. For the next week, keep a journal on the times when you feel exhausted. Reflect on your day and ask yourself what you did and whether you overtaxed yourself.

5. Wattles encourages that if you are in a business that beats people in the competitive sense (versus the creative sense), get out at once. Does your business do so? If not, have you ever been in a business that does? Write about the details of the business and how you felt being a part of it.

6. Wattles asserts that you should "Give every man more in use value than you take from him in cash value." Have you being doing so in your business? How might you be able to enhance your customers' experience so that they receive more from you?

7. Your business should be filled with the principle of advancement, so that each employee who wishes to do so may advance a little every day. How might you be able to help your coworkers advance each day? Write down three ideas, and then begin to implement them. Take note of any energetic changes you feel.

8. What ladders do you have in place for fellow employees at your business? Write a list of the existing ladders that you have in place.

9. Desire and absolute faith that what you wish for is coming to you via Thinking Substance are keys to manifesting. Has there been anything you have desired in your life that you had absolute faith would manifest, and it did? Write about your experience in as much detail as possible.

10. Is there anything that you have absolute faith in is coming your way in your life? If so, write about it, using all of your senses and in great detail.

11. "You need not hesitate about asking largely . . . 'it is your Father's pleasure to give you the kingdom' said Jesus." Do you struggle with asking for large-scale abundance

in your life? If so, write a list of why you find asking for a great deal of abundance difficult.

12. What if you knew for certain that to the Thinking Substance, creating a carrot takes the same energy as creating one million dollars? The difference only lies in your perception. Take a moment to let this sink into your psyche. Knowing that all is created with equal ease, write a new list of any additional things that you would like to manifest in your life.

13. Wattles shares the story of the boy who so desperately wanted to play the piano. The boy said that he could feel the music, but just couldn't get his hands to go right. Have you ever experienced a deep desire, but like the boy, struggled with "how" to make that desire unfold? Write about at least one such desire you have had.

14. The author asserts that the One Substance or God is trying to live, do, and enjoy things through humanity; that we are the divine expression incarnate. This would then include expressing the joy of receiving and having. With this powerful new understanding, you would see that being and dreaming small does not serve you or the divine. Write a list of how you might better serve the One Substance through your talents, your joys, and wants that are manifested.

15. At the end of this chapter Wattles shares a delightful and inspiring story about a very poor student who started small, but grew in his ability to manifest his desires in the form of a home. What about this story touches your heart? Replay the story in your head, shifting the main character from the student to you. Imagine yourself manifesting piece-by-piece all of the abundance that you desire. Once you have fully felt into your visualization with

all of your senses, write about it in as much detail as possible.

16. Wattles shares how the student began living "in the Certain Way." Reflect on your current state of mind and practices. How are you not living in the Certain Way?

17. Make another list of how you are living in the Certain Way.

18. Make a new list of the things you can do and feel so that you are living in the Certain Way. Be sure to do and feel the things that you listed on a regular basis over a prolonged period of time. Keep a journal that records any noted changes your life.

Chapter 7

Gratitude

The illustrations given in the last chapter will have conveyed to the reader the fact that the first step toward getting rich is to convey the idea of your wants to the Formless Substance. This is true, and you will see that in order to do so it becomes necessary to relate yourself to the Formless Intelligence in a harmonious way. To secure this harmonious relation is a matter of such primary and vital importance that I shall give some space to its discussion here, and give you instructions which, if you will follow them, will be certain to bring you into perfect unity of mind with God. The whole process of mental adjustment and atonement can be summed up in one word, gratitude.

First, you believe that there is one Intelligent Substance, from which all things proceed; second, you believe that this Substance gives you everything you desire; and third, you relate yourself to it by a feeling of deep and profound gratitude. Many people who order their lives rightly in all other ways are kept in poverty by their lack of gratitude. Having received one gift from God, they cut the wires which connect them with Him by failing to make acknowledgment.

It is easy to understand that the nearer we live to the source of wealth, the more wealth we shall receive; and it is easy also to understand that the soul that is always grateful lives in closer touch with God than the one which never looks to Him in thankful acknowledgment. The more gratefully we fix our minds on the Supreme when good things come to us, the more good things we will receive, and the more rapidly they will come; and the reason simply is that the mental attitude of gratitude draws the mind into closer touch with the source from which the blessings come. If it is a new thought to you that gratitude brings your whole mind into closer harmony with the creative energies of the universe, consider it well, and you will see that it is true. The good things you already have have come to you along the line of obedience to certain laws. Gratitude will lead your mind out along the ways by which things come; and it will keep you in close harmony with creative thought and prevent you from falling into competitive thought.

Gratitude alone can keep you looking toward the All, and prevent you from falling into the error of thinking of the supply as limited; and to do that would be fatal to your hopes. There is a Law of Gratitude, and it is absolutely necessary that you should observe the law, if you are to get the results you seek. The law of gratitude is the natural principle that action and reaction are always equal, and in opposite directions.

The grateful outreaching of your mind in thankful praise to the Supreme is a liberation or expenditure of force; it cannot fail to reach that to which it addressed, and the reaction is an instantaneous movement towards you. "Draw nigh unto God, and He will draw nigh unto you." That is a statement of psychological truth. And if your gratitude is strong and constant, the reaction in Formless Substance will be strong and continuous; the movement of the things you want will be always toward you. Notice the grateful attitude that Jesus took; how He always seems to be saying, "I thank Thee, Father, that Thou hearest me." You cannot exercise much power without gratitude; for it is gratitude that keeps you connected with Power.

But the value of gratitude does not consist solely in getting you more blessings in the future. Without gratitude you cannot long keep from dissatisfied thought regarding things as they are. The moment you permit your mind to dwell with dissatisfaction upon things as they are, you begin to lose ground. You fix attention upon the common, the ordinary, the poor, and the squalid and mean; and your mind takes the form of these things. Then you will transmit these forms or mental images to the Formless, and the common, the poor, the squalid, and mean will come to you.

To permit your mind to dwell upon the inferior is to become inferior and to surround yourself with inferior things. On the other hand, to fix your attention on the best is to surround yourself with the best, and to become the best. The Creative Power within us makes us into the image of that to which we give our attention. We are Thinking Substance, and thinking substance always takes the form of that which it thinks about. The grateful mind is constantly fixed upon the best; therefore it tends to become the best; it takes the form or character of the best, and will receive the best.

Also, faith is born of gratitude. The grateful mind continually expects good things, and expectation becomes faith. The reaction of gratitude upon one's own mind produces faith; and every outgoing wave of grateful thanksgiving increases faith. He who has no feeling of gratitude cannot long retain a living faith; and without a living faith you cannot get rich by the creative method, as we shall see in the following chapters. It is necessary, then, to cultivate the habit of being grateful for every good thing that comes to you; and to give thanks continuously. And because all things have contributed to your advancement, you should include all things in your gratitude.

Do not waste time thinking or talking about the shortcomings or wrong actions of plutocrats or trust magnates. Their organization of the world has made your opportunity; all you get really comes to you because of them. Do not rage against, corrupt politicians; if it were not for politicians we should fall into anarchy, and your opportunity would be greatly lessened. God has worked a long time and very patiently to bring us up to where we are in industry and government, and He is going right on with His work. There is not the least doubt that He will do away with plutocrats, trust magnates, captains of industry, and politicians as soon as they can be spared;

but in the meantime, behold they are all very good. Remember that they are ll helping to arrange the lines of transmission along which your riches will come to you, and be grateful to them all. This will bring you into harmonious relations with the good in everything, and the good in everything will move toward you.

STUDY GUIDE

Gratitude

1. Wallace Wattles opens this chapter emphasizing that you must relate yourself to the Formless Intelligence in a harmonious way. This references being in perfect unity with the mind of God. On a scale from one to ten (one being "very little" and ten being "a great deal"), how much in harmony with the mind of God do you believe yourself to be?

1——2——3——4——5——6——7——8——9——10

2. Gratitude is the key to atonement. Wattles lists the three steps as:
   • Believe that there is one Intelligent Substance;
   • Believe that this Substance gives you everything you desire;
   • Relate yourself to it by a feeling of deep and profound gratitude.

   Go through each of the steps and rate where you currently are with each (1=least; 10=most):

   Believe that there is one Intelligent Substance:

   1——2——3——4——5——6——7——8——9——10

   Believe that this Substance gives you everything you desire:

   1——2——3——4——5——6——7——8——9——10

Relate yourself to it by a feeling of deep and profound gratitude.

1———2———3———4———5———6———7———8———9———10

3. Failing to make acknowledgment to the Intelligent Substance cuts the wires that connect you to it. Reflect on your life, and take some time to acknowledge all of the gifts that you have received. Start with your childhood and work your way forward to present day.

4. How did you feel after doing the exercise in number 3 above?

5. For the rest of today and moving forward, make a conscious commitment to finding gratitude, even for the little things in your life. Start a Gratitude Journal and keep it with you. You may want a small notebook that you can keep in your pocket. Each time you note something you appreciate, write down a gratitude statement in response to it.

6. Wattles states ". . . the mental attitude of gratitude draws the mind into closer touch with the source from which the blessings come." When practicing your gratitude journal, make note of any changes you experience in relation to doing this exercise. Do you feel more connected to God or Intelligent Substance?

7. Practicing gratitude gets your mind out of competitive thought and in closer harmony with creative thought. Take an inventory after one month of writing in your Gratitude Journal. Are you feeling less competitive? If not, check in with yourself. Are you enjoying and appreciating doing the journal, or is it more an act of obedience?

8. If you are not enjoying the practice of writing in your Gratitude Journal, give yourself time to feel into the experience

of gratitude with each entry you make into it. Really feel into the gratitude and joy of the experiences for which you are grateful.

9. According to Wattles, "The grateful outreaching of your mind in thankful praise to the Supreme is a liberation or expenditure of force; it cannot fail to reach that to which it addressed, and the reaction is an instantaneous movement towards you." Write down the ways in which you have noticed "movement" towards you in response to maintaining your Gratitude Journal.

10. If your gratitude is strong and constant, the reaction in Formless Substance will be strong and continuous. How might you develop a strong and constant gratitude? Besides the journal, practice waking up each morning and lying in bed for a couple of extra moments. Reflect upon all in your life that you are grateful for. Also, before going to sleep each night, again reflect on your day and all that you appreciated about it.

11. The moment you permit your mind to dwell with dissatisfaction upon things as they are, you fix your attention upon the common, the ordinary, the poor, and the squalid and mean. Your mind takes the form of these things. Ultimately they will come to you. Think of a time that you were caught in a web of negative thinking. Did you find yourself experiencing one negativity after another? Write about the experience.

12. Write a statement or declaration of gratitude in response to the negative experience that you just shared. Write about the fact that you now see its effect and no longer choose to focus on negativity in your life.

13. "Thinking substance always takes the form of that which it thinks about. The grateful mind is constantly fixed upon the best; therefore it tends to become the best . . . and will receive the best." Explain why this statement is true, citing examples to back up your explanation.

14. Wattles explains that faith is born of gratitude. If you have been lacking faith in your ability to have your desires manifest, perhaps gratitude has been the missing link. On a scale from one to ten (one being "very little" and ten being "a great deal"), rate how faithful you are that you will attain the abundance you desire.

1——2——3——4——5——6——7——8——9——10

15. You are encouraged not to waste time thinking of short-comings, nor rage against corrupt politicians. You should be grateful to them all, for they are all helping to arrange the lines of transmission. Briefly reflect on the businesses, politicians, individuals, cultures or other entities that you struggle with, judging as corrupt or having other short-comings. Write down some ways that will help you shift your focus away from them, and towards more empower-ing topics a bit more each day.

16. Once you have completed your list in #15, write a grat-itude statement of appreciation about each entry you have listed.

Chapter 8

Thinking In The Certain Way

Turn back to chapter 6 (page 61), and read again the story of the man who formed a mental image of his house, and you will get a fair idea of the initial step toward getting rich. You must form a clear and definite mental picture of what you want; you cannot transmit an idea unless you have it yourself. You must have it before you can give it; and many people fail to impress Thinking Substance because they have themselves only a vague and misty concept of the things they want to do, to have, or to become. It is not enough that you should have a general desire for wealth "to do good with"; everybody has that desire.

It is not enough that you should have a wish to travel, see things, live more, etc. Everybody has those desires also. If you were going to send a wireless message to a friend, you would not send the letters of the alphabet in their order, and let him construct the message for himself; nor would you take words at random from the dictionary. You would send a coherent sentence; one which meant something. When you try to impress your wants upon Substance, remember that it must be done by a coherent statement; you must know what you want, and be definite. You can never get rich, or start the creative power into action, by sending out unformed longings and vague desires.

Go over your desires just as the man I have described went over his house; see just what you want, and get a clear mental picture of it as you wish it to look when you get it. That clear mental picture you must have continually in mind, as the sailor has in mind the port toward which he is sailing the ship; you must keep your face toward it all the time. You must no more lose sight of it than the steersman loses sight of the compass.

It is not necessary to take exercises in concentration, nor to set apart special times for prayer and affirmation, nor to "go into the silence," nor to do occult stunts of any kind. There things are well enough, but all you need is to know what you want, and to want it badly enough so that it will stay in your thoughts.

Spend as much of your leisure time as you can in contemplating your picture, but no one needs to take exercises to concentrate his mind on a thing which he really wants; it is the things you do not really care about which require effort to fix your attention upon them. And unless you really want to get rich, so that the desire is strong enough to hold your thoughts directed to the purpose as the magnetic pole holds the needle of the compass, it will hardly be worth while for you to try to carry out the instructions given in this book.

The methods herein set forth are for people whose desire for riches is strong enough to overcome mental laziness and the love of ease, and make them work. The more clear and definite you make your picture then, and the more you dwell upon it, bringing out all its delightful details, the stronger your desire will be; and the stronger your desire, the easier it will be to hold your mind fixed upon the picture of what you want. Something more is necessary, however, than merely to see the picture clearly. If that is all you do, you are only a dreamer, and will have little or no power for accomplishment.

Behind your clear vision must be the purpose to realize it; to bring it out in tangible expression. And behind this purpose must be an invincible and unwavering FAITH that the thing is already yours; that it is "at hand" and you have only to take possession of it.

Live in the new house, mentally, until it takes form around you physically. In the mental realm, enter at once into full enjoyment of the things you want. "Whatsoever things ye ask for when ye pray, believe that ye receive them, and ye shall have them," said Jesus. See the things you want as if they were actually around you all the time; see yourself as owning and using them. Make use of them in imagination just as you will use them when they are your tangible possessions. Dwell upon your mental picture until it is clear and distinct, and then take the Mental Attitude of Ownership toward everything in that picture. Take possession of it, in mind, in the full faith that it is actually yours. Hold to this mental ownership; do not waiver for an instant in the faith that it is real. And remember what was said in a proceeding chapter about gratitude; be as thankful for it all the time as you expect to be when it has taken form. The man who can sincerely thank God for the things which as yet he owns only in imagination, has real faith. He will get rich; he will cause the creation of whatsoever he wants.

You do not need to pray repeatedly for things you want; it is not necessary to tell God about it every day. "Use not vain repetitions as the heathen do," said Jesus said to his pupils, "for your Father knoweth the ye have need of these things before ye ask Him."

Your part is to intelligently formulate your desire for the things which make for a larger life, and to get these desire arranged into a coherent whole; and then to impress this Whole Desire upon the Formless Substance, which has the power and the will to bring you what you want. You do not make this impression by repeating strings of words; you make it by holding the vision with unshakable PURPOSE to attain it, and with steadfast FAITH that you do attain it.

The answer to prayer is not according to your faith while you are talking, but according to your faith while you are working. You cannot impress the mind of God by having a special Sabbath day set apart to tell Him what you want, and the forgetting Him during the rest of the week. You cannot impress Him by having special hours to go into your closet and pray, if you then dismiss the matter from your mind until the hour of prayer comes again.

Oral prayer is well enough, and has its effect, especially upon yourself, in clarifying your vision and strengthening your faith; but it is not your oral petitions which get you what you want. In order to get rich you do not need a "sweet hour of prayer"; you need to "pray without ceasing." And by prayer I mean holding steadily to your vision, with the purpose to cause its creation into solid form, and the faith that you are doing so.

The whole matter turns on receiving, once you have clearly formed your vision. When you have formed it, it is well to make an oral statement, addressing the Supreme in reverent prayer; and from that moment you must, in mind, receive what you ask for. Live in the new house; wear the fine clothes; ride in the automobile; go on the journey, and confidently plan for greater journeys. Think and speak of all the things you have asked for in terms of actual present ownership. Imagine an environment, and a financial condition exactly as you want them, and live all the time in that imaginary environment and financial condition. Mind, however, that you do not do this as a mere dreamer and castle builder; hold to the FAITH that the imaginary is being realized, and to the PURPOSE to realize it. Remember that it is faith and purpose in the use of the imagination which make the difference between the scientist and the dreamer. And having learned this fact, it is here that you must learn the proper use of the Will.

STUDY GUIDE

Thinking In the Certain Way

1. Wattles opens this chapter by reasserting that you must form a clean and definite mental picture of what you want. He explains that it is not enough to have a vague and misty concept of your desires. Review the previous descriptions of what you desire, and then visualize a perfect day in your future; experiencing all that you desire. Before doing the visualization, set your intention to find even more specific sensing details than previous visualizations.

2. Write the visualization, being sure to include the additional details that you experienced and communicated to the Thinking Substance.

3. Whiles Wattles claims that you need not do anything special to manifest your desires, all you need do is to want them badly enough so that they will stay in your thoughts. On a scale from one to ten (one being "very little" and ten being "a great deal"), rate how keenly you really want to manifest your desires in your life.

1——2——3——4——5——6——7——8——9——10

4. Wattles states that, "Behind your clear vision must be the purpose to realize it; to bring it out in tangible expression . . . and behind this purpose must be an invincible and unwavering FAITH that the thing is already yours; that it is 'at hand'; all you have only to take possession of

it." Do you have an unwavering faith that all you desire is in the ethers, awaiting your readiness for it to manifest? Describe your thoughts and feelings around this premise.

5. "The man who can sincerely thank God for the things which as yet he owns only in imagination, has real faith." If you haven't already done so, take time to thank God for that which is to eventually come into your life. Make a practice of gratitude in anticipation of what is to be.

6. "Your part is to intelligently formulate your desire for the things which make for a larger life, and to get these desires arranged into a coherent whole." Do you have your desires arranged into a coherent whole? Do you see details like: how much money is in your bank account; how you spend your day; the individuals who you assist with your success; how your success affects the world and those around you? Take some time to review your written desires and visualizations, and then fill in more detail. Organize them into a coherent whole.

7. *"In order to get rich you do not need a 'sweet hour of prayer'; you need to 'pray without ceasing' . . . holding steadily to your vision, with the purpose to cause its creation into solid form, and the faith that you are doing so."* You need to believe that you will receive them. Do you hold a constant vision of manifesting the abundance that you desire, or is it a "sometimes" exercise? If you haven't already done so, put photographs or notes about what you wish to manifest in your bathroom, bedroom, on the refrigerator door, on your desk, etc. Keep constant reminders of what you desire to manifest around you so that seeing it and believing it becomes a constant in your life.

8. Once you have clearly formed your vision of what you want, make an oral statement, "addressing the Supreme

in reverent prayer." Take some time to write your prayer, and then say it aloud with the confidence that it is heard and will manifest. Be sure not to speak it in a begging or questioning manner, for doing so does not reflect the energy of faith and knowing.

9. Now it is time for you to "think and speak of all the things you have asked for in terms of actual present ownership." From this point forward, be sure to reference your desires in the now. "I have" versus "I want." For the next week, make note of any times when you speak from I wish, I want, etc. and change the statement to an affirmative, "I have."

10. Wattles states that the difference between a dreamer and a scientist is faith and purpose in the use of the imagination. If you simply dream about your desires in a flighty and whimsical way, but do not hold the faith that they will manifest, you have not mastered the science of manifesting abundance. Take a couple of moments to imagine having your desires manifest. Are you a whimsical dreamer or is there commitment and trust in your imagining?

Chapter 9

How To Use The Will

To set about getting rich in a scientific way, you do not try to apply your will power to anything outside of yourself. You have no right to do so, anyway. It is wrong to apply your will to other men and women, in order to get them to do what you wish done.

It is as flagrantly wrong to coerce people by mental power as it is to coerce them by physical power. If compelling people by physical force to do things for you reduces them to slavery, compelling them by mental means accomplishes exactly the same thing; the only difference is in methods. If taking things from people by physical force is robbery, them taking things by mental force is robbery also; there is no difference in principle.

You have no right to use your will power upon another person, even "for his own good"; for you do not know what is for his good. The science of getting rich does not require you to apply power or force to any other person, in any way whatsoever. There is not the slightest necessity for doing so; indeed, any attempt to use your will upon others will only tend to defeat your purpose. You do not need to apply your will to things, in order to compel them to come to you.

That would simply be trying to coerce God, and would be foolish and useless, as well as irreverent. You do not have to compel God to give you good things, any more than you have to use your will power to make the sun rise. You do not have to use your will power to conquer an unfriendly deity, or to make stubborn and rebellious forces do your bidding. Substance is friendly to you, and is more anxious to give you what you want than you are to get it. To get rich, you need only to use your will power upon yourself.

When you know what to think and do, then you must use your will to compel yourself to think and do the right things. That is the legitimate use of the will in getting what you want—to use it in holding yourself to the right course. Use your will to keep yourself thinking and acting in the Certain Way. Do not try to project your will, or your thoughts, or your mind out into space, to "act" on things or people. Keep your mind at home; it can accomplish more there than elsewhere. Use your mind to form a mental image of what you want, and to hold that vision with faith and purpose; and use your will to keep your mind working in the Right Way. The more steady and continuous your faith and purpose, the more rapidly you will get rich, because you will make only POSITIVE impressions upon Substance; and you will not neutralize or offset them by negative impressions.

The picture of your desires, held with faith and purpose, is taken up by the Formless, and permeates it to great distances-throughout the universe, for all I know. As this impression spreads, all things are set moving toward its realization; every living thing, every inanimate thing, and the things yet uncreated, are stirred toward bringing into being that which you want. All force begins to be exerted in that direction; all things begin to move toward you. The minds of people, everywhere, are influenced toward doing the things necessary to the fulfilling of your desires; and they work for you, unconsciously.

But you can check all this by starting a negative impression in the Formless Substance. Doubt or unbelief is as certain to start a movement away from you as faith and purpose are to start one toward you. It is by not understanding this that most people who try to make use of "mental science" in getting rich make their failure. Every hour and moment you spend in giving heed to doubts and fears, every hour you spend in worry, every hour in which your soul is possessed by unbelief, sets a current away from you in the whole domain of intelligent Substance. All the promises are unto them that believe, and unto them only. Notice how insistent Jesus was upon this point of belief; and now you know the reason why.

Since belief is all important, it behooves you to guard your thoughts; and as your beliefs will be shaped to a very great extent by the things you observe and think about, it is important that you should command your attention. And here the will comes into use; for it is by your will that you determine upon what things your attention shall be fixed. If you want to become rich, you must not make a study of poverty. Things are not brought into being by thinking about their opposites. Health is never to be attained by studying disease and thinking about disease; righteousness is not to be promoted by studying sin and thinking about sin; and no one ever got rich by studying poverty and thinking about poverty. Medicine as a science of disease has increased disease; religion as a science of sin has promoted sin, and economics as a study of poverty will fill the world with wretchedness and want.

Do not talk about poverty; do not investigate it, or concern yourself with it. Never mind what its causes are; you have nothing to do with them. What concerns you is the cure. Do not spend your time in charitable work, or charity movements; all charity only tends to perpetuate the wretchedness it aims to eradicate. I do not say that you should be hard hearted or unkind, and refuse to hear the cry of need; but you must not try to eradicate poverty in any of the conventional ways. Put poverty behind you, and put all that pertains to it behind you, and "make good." Get rich; that is the best way you can help the poor.

And you cannot hold the mental image which is to make you rich if you fill your mind with pictures of poverty. Do not read books or papers which give circumstantial accounts of the wretchedness of the tenement dwellers, 41 of the horrors of child labor, and so on. Do not read anything which fills your mind with gloomy images of want and suffering. You cannot help the poor in the least by knowing about these things; and the wide-spread knowledge of them does not tend at all to do away with poverty.

What tends to do away with poverty is not the getting of pictures of poverty into your mind, but getting pictures of wealth into the minds of the poor. You are not deserting the poor in their misery when you refuse to allow your mind to be filled with pictures of that misery. Poverty can be done away with, not by increasing the number of well to do people who think about poverty, but by increasing the number of poor people who purpose with faith to get rich. The poor do not need charity; they need inspiration. Charity only sends them a loaf of bread to keep them alive in their wretchedness, or gives them an entertainment to make them forget for an hour or two; but inspiration will cause them to rise out of their misery. If you want to help the poor, demonstrate to them that they can become rich; prove it by getting rich yourself.

The only way in which poverty will ever be banished from this world is by getting a large and constantly increasing number of people to practice the teachings of this book. People must be taught to become rich by creation, not by competition. Every man who becomes rich by competition throws down behind him the ladder by which he rises, and keeps others down; but every man who gets rich by creation opens a way for thousands to follow him, and inspires them to do so.

You are not showing hardness of heart or an unfeeling disposition when you refuse to pity poverty, see poverty, read about poverty, or think or talk about it, or to listen to those who do talk about it. Use your will power to keep your mind OFF the subject of poverty, and to keep it fixed with faith and purpose ON the vision of what you want.

STUDY GUIDE

How to Use the Will

1. Wattles opens this chapter by suggesting that you do not try to apply your will power to anything outside yourself; that you have no right to do so. Reflect on your life. Write a list of situations in which you find yourself trying to control things outside of yourself. What people do you try to change? What situations do you try to alter? Be as honest and as thorough as possible.

2. It is just as wrong to coerce people by mental power, as it is to do so with physical force. Go back to the list of people you created in #1. For each individual, see yourself releasing them to their own control. Feel the peace in this energy shift. Feel the power in no longer being responsible for their choices or behavior.

3. Trying to apply your will in order to compel them to come to you would simply be trying to coerce God. Reflect on your past beliefs and actions. Have you been trying to will things to you, not completing trusting that the divine is already doing so? Write about any new insights you gain as you explore coercion and how it has shown up in your life.

4. Wattles states that "Substance is friendly to you, and is more anxious to give you what you want than you are to get it." Do you truly believe this statement? Speak it aloud. How do you feel when you say it? Write about your feelings.

5. The only will power you should use is to compel yourself to think and do the right things, to use it to hold yourself on the right course. Where have you struggled with your will power waning? Have you struggled with the choice of foods you eat? With practicing regular exercise? With cultivating a routine meditation or contemplation practice? Write a list of the areas where you struggle to "think and do the right things" for yourself.

6. If any of the items that you just listed relates to your manifesting of abundance goals, write it down and write an action plan on how you will follow through on holding yourself on the right course.

7. Write about any findings or shifts that you note in relation to completing #5 and #6.

8. Wattles states, "Keep your mind at home; it can accomplish more there than elsewhere." Pay attention to where your mind wanders elsewhere—away from home. Keep a list of where your mind wanders, and see if there is a theme to the list. For example, does your mind wander when you are starting to feel good and on track? Does it wander when you are feeling stressed or overwhelmed?

9. Now take note of what you think of when your mind wanders. Are there any themes to where you go when your mind wanders? If so, write them down and any new insights you may have gathered by doing this exercise.

10. It is suggested that you use your mind to form a mental image of what you want. How long can you hold onto that image? Does your mind wander when you focus it on that which you desire? If so, what thoughts come up that distract you from envisioning your desires. Record and track them.

11. "The more steady and continuous your faith and purpose, the more rapidly you will get rich, because you will make only POSITIVE impressions upon Substance; and you will not neutralize or offset them by negative impressions." With this statement, it appears that energy is a balancing game. The more you direct positive impressions upon Substance, the less you can offset them by negative impressions. What percentage of your thoughts would you say are:

    Negative _____   Positive _____   Neutral _____

12. What percentage would you realistically and ideally want your thoughts to be?

    Negative _____   Positive _____   Neutral _____

13. According to Wattles, all things will begin to move towards you, even the minds of people, everywhere; they work for you unconsciously. When you hear this, do you carry any doubt? If so, write about it.

14. For at least five minutes, contemplate the idea that all others in the world are working towards assisting you in manifesting your greatest desires. Imagine seeing energy radiating from everyone that sends positive energy towards you and all that you want. Once you have completed visualizing this, write about the feelings that you experienced while doing the exercise.

15. "Every hour and moment you spend in giving heed to doubts and fears, every hour you spend in worry, every hour in which your soul is possessed by unbelief, sets a current away from you in the whole domain of intelligent Substance." How much time do you spend worrying in your life, and what do you worry about? For the next week, note each time you catch yourself worrying about

something or someone. You will likely find that the worry often continues on the same theme(s) and is repetitive.

16. Write a list of how worrying affects you. Are there any positive ways that it impacts you? Are there any negative ways that it impacts you? Please list them.

17. Wattles states, "If you want to become rich, you must not make a study of poverty." Do you spend much time studying or thinking about poverty? If so, what percentage of your time do you spend doing so? What might you do to lessen your focus on poverty?

18. According to Wattles, "Medicine as a science of disease has increased disease; religion as a science of sin has promoted sin." Do you worry about or focus on disease and unhealthiness? How much attention do you give to the multitude of commercials that speak about diseases, medications and all of their side effects?

19. Do you watch the news and focus on the negativity that the media covers so frequently? Try to turn your television off for at least two weeks. Stay away from the news on the radio and Internet. Take note of how this affects your attitude and your energy. Write about any insights you gain by doing so. If you could not practice this exercise, why not? What were you unwilling to give up? What were you afraid of?

20. Wattles claims that you should not focus your energy on charitable work, as doing so only perpetuates the wretchedness it aims to eradicate. He claims that you would "make good" by putting poverty and all that pertains to it behind you. The best way you can help the poor is to get rich. Some might have problem with this suggestion.

How might this counter the teachings that you have integrated into your life?

21. Wattles claims that getting pictures of wealth into the minds of the poor is the best way to rid the world of poverty. Do you believe this to be so? Explain.

22. Wattles writes, "Every man who becomes rich by competition throws down behind him the ladder by which he rises, and keeps others down; but every man who gets rich by creation opens a way for thousands to follow him, and inspires them to do so." Have you ever considered that becoming rich is your responsibility and duty towards paving the way to success for others? Write about how your eventual wealth will help others in the world; not just through philanthropy, but by your modeling and mentoring.

23. At the end of this chapter you are encouraged to stay away from anything to do with poverty. Is there anything in your home or in your life that reflects or reminds you of poverty? If so, get rid of it.

Chapter 10

Further Use Of The Will

You cannot retain a true and clear vision of wealth if you are constantly turning your attention to opposing pictures, whether they be external or imaginary. Do not tell of your past troubles of a financial nature, if you have had them, do not think of them at all. Do no tell of the poverty of your parents, or the hardships of your early life; to do any of these things is to mentally class yourself with the poor for the time being, and it will certainly check the movement of things in your direction.

"Let the dead bury their dead," as Jesus said. Put poverty and all things that pertain to poverty completely behind you. You have accepted a certain theory of the universe as being correct, and are resting all your hopes of happiness on its being correct; and what can you gain by giving heed to conflicting theories? Do not read religious books which tell you that the world is soon coming to an end; and do not read the writing of muck-rakers and pessimistic philosophers who tell you that it is going to the devil. The world is not going to the devil; it is going to God. It is wonderful Becoming.

True, there may be a good many things in existing conditions which are disagreeable; but what is the use of studying them when they are certainly passing away, and when the study of them only tends to check their passing and keep them with us? Why give time and attention to things which are being removed by evolutionary growth, when you can hasten their removal only by promoting the evolutionary growth as far as your part of it goes? No matter how horrible in seeming may be the conditions in certain countries, sections, or places, you waste your time and destroy your own chances by considering them. You should interest yourself in the world's becoming rich.

Think of the riches the world is coming into, instead of the poverty it is growing out of; and bear in mind that the only way in which you can assist the world in growing rich is by growing rich yourself through the creative method—not the competitive one. Give your attention wholly to riches; ignore poverty. Whenever you think or speak of those who are poor, think and speak of them as those who are becoming rich;as those who are to be congratulated rather than pitied. Then they and others will catch the inspiration, and begin to search for the way out.

Because I say that you are to give your whole time and mind and thought to riches, it does not follow that you are to be sordid or mean. To become really rich is the noblest aim you can have in life, for it includes everything else. On the competitive plane, the struggle to get rich is a Godless scramble for power over other men; but when we come into the creative mind, all this is changed.

All that is possible in the way of greatness and soul unfoldment, of service and lofty endeavor, comes by way of getting rich; all is made possible by the use of things. If you lack for physical health, you will find that the attainment of it is conditional on your getting rich. Only those who are emancipated from financial worry, and who have the means to live a care-free existence and follow hygienic practices, can have and retain health.

Moral and spiritual greatness is possible only to those who are above the competitive battle for existence; and only those who are becoming rich on the plane of creative thought are free from the degrading influences of competition. If your heart is set on domestic happiness, remember that love flourishes best where there is refinement, a high level of thought, and freedom from corrupting influences; and these are to be found only where riches are attained by the exercise of creative thought, without strife or rivalry.

You can aim at nothing so great or noble, I repeat, as to become rich; and you must fix your attention upon your mental picture of riches, to the exclusion of all that may tend to dim or obscure the vision. You must learn to see the underlying TRUTH in all things; you must see beneath all seemingly wrong conditions the Great One Life ever moving forward toward fuller expression and more complete happiness. It is the truth that there is no such thing as poverty; that there is only wealth. Some people remain in poverty because they are ignorant of the fact that there is wealth for them; and these can best be taught by showing them the way to affluence in your own person and practice. Others are poor because, while they feel that there is a way out, they are too intellectually indolent to put forth the mental effort necessary to find that way and by travel it; and for these the very best thing you can do is to arouse their desire by showing them the happiness that comes from being rightly rich.

Others still are poor because, while they have some notion of science, they have become so swamped and lost in the maze of metaphysical and occult theories that they do not know which road to take. They try a mixture of many systems and fail in all. For these, again, the very best thing, to do is to show the right way in your own person and practice; an ounce of doing things is worth a pound of theorizing.

The very best thing you can do for the whole world is to make the most of yourself. You can serve God and man in no more effective way than by getting rich; that is, if you get rich by the creative method and not by the competetive one. Another thing. We assert that this book gives in detail the principles of the science of getting rich; and if that is true, you do not need to read any other book upon the subject. This may sound narrow and egotistical, but consider: there is no more scientific method of computation in mathematics than by addition, subtraction, multiplication, and division; no other method is possible. There can be but one shortest distance between two points. There is only one way to think scientifically, and that is to think in the way that leads by the most direct and simple route to the goal. No man has yet formulated a briefer or less complex "system" than the one set forth herein; it has been stripped of all non-essentials. When you commence on this, lay all others aside; put them out of your mind altogether.

Read this book every day; keep it with you; commit it to memory, and do not think about other "systems" and theories. If you do, you will begin to have doubts, and to be uncertain and wavering in your thought; and then you will begin to make failures. After you have made good and become rich, you may study other systems as much as you please; but until you are quite sure that you have gained what you want, do not read anything on this line but this book, unless it be the authors mentioned in the Preface. And read only the most optimistic comments on the world's news; those in harmony with your picture.

Also, postpone your investigations into the occult. Do not dabble in theosophy, Spiritualism, or kindred studies. It is very likely that the dead still live, and are near; but if they are, let them alone; mind your own business. Wherever the spirits of the dead may be, they have their own work to do, and their own problems to solve; and we have no right to interfere with them. We cannot help them, and it is very doubtful whether they can help us, or whether we have any right to trespass upon their time if they can. Let the dead and the hereafter alone, and solve your own problem; get rich. If you begin to mix with the occult, you will start mental cross-currents which will surely bring your hopes to shipwreck. Now, this and the preceding chapters have brought us to the following statement of basic facts:

There is a thinking stuff from which all things are made, and which, in its original state, permeates, penetrates, and fills the interspaces of the universe. A thought, in this substance, Produces the thing that is imaged by the thought. Man can form things in his thought, and, by impressing his thought upon formless substance, can cause the thing he thinks about to be created. In order to do this, man must pass from the competitive to the creative mind; he must form a clear mental picture of the things he wants, and hold this picture in his thoughts with the fixed PURPOSE to get what he wants, and the unwavering FAITH that he does get what he wants, closing his mind against all that may tend to shake his purpose, dim his vision, or quench his faith. And in addition to all this, we shall now see that he must live and act in a Certain Way.

Further Use Of the Will

1. Wattles opens this chapter warning you not to tell of your past troubles of a financial nature. Put all things that pertain to poverty behind you. Do you tend towards telling stories of lack from your childhood, or your parents' poverty- stricken lives? If so, make a point to put it all behind you. As you feel a story of the past well up inside you, refrain from speaking it and make a conscious choice to focus your thoughts on your future of abundance.

2. You are encouraged to stay away from pessimistic philosophers who tell you that the world is coming to an end. The movie theaters are filled with catastrophic "end of the world" movies. Write a list of those you have viewed. Then do a practice of some kind to lift the dark energy from your psyche. Burn the list, or throw it away, stating that there is no room for such negativity in your life. If you have viewed these types of movies in the past, make a new choice to stay away from them.

3. Wattles encourages you to interest yourself in the world's becoming rich, and staying away from focusing on the horrible conditions that exist in certain countries. Write a list of books, magazines or other periodicals where you could find information on ways in which the world is becoming rich. Then make a point of researching them and filling your mind with all the good that is manifesting in the world.

4. How might you focus on the poor becoming rich? Write an example.

5. To become really rich is the noblest aim you can have in life. How so? Write about how your unique situation reflects your nobility in making the choice to become rich.

6. The author states that, "If you lack for physical health, you will find that the attainment of it is conditional on your getting rich." How is your physical health? If you haven't had a recent physical, book an appointment for one.

7. If you have any health issues, practice seeing yourself in complete wholeness, which is your true natural state. Write about any insights you gain in repositioning your perspective.

8. Why would Wattles state that, "Moral and spiritual greatness is possible only to those who are above the competitive battle for existence"? In other words, why would one not be able to compete and maintain moral and spiritual greatness? Isn't natural competition a healthy part of the human experience? If not, why not?

9. According to the author, "Love flourishes best where there is refinement, a high level of thought, and freedom from corrupting influences; and these are to be found only where riches are attained by the exercise of creative thought, without strife or rivalry." Do you believe that you cannot be without strife or rivalry if you are poor? If not, why not?

10. Wattles says that you must see beneath all seemingly wrong conditions. Have you ever experienced what appeared to be a setback, only to discover that it was a blessing in disguise? Write about such an occurrence in

your life. If you can't think of one in your life, write about such a case in another's life.

11. Wattles says that some people remain in poverty because they are ignorant of the fact that there is wealth for them, and that you can best teach them by showing them the way. Reflect on your life and think of at least one person that you believe is in lack consciousness. Now imagine yourself manifesting the abundance that you desire, and showing them another way. How does this make you feel? Write about your experience and feelings in relation to it.

12. You can show others the happiness that comes from being rightly rich, by being rightly rich. Write a list of individuals for whom you could be a model by attaining abundance. Then imagine each of them following your lead and thanking you for modeling the way for them. Then write about your experience in as much detail as possible.

13. "An ounce of doing things is worth a pound of theorizing." How much "doing" do you practice, as opposed to theorizing? On a scale from one to ten (one being "very little" and ten being "a great deal"), rate how much theorizing you do.

1——2——3——4——5——6——7——8——9——10

14. On a scale from one to ten (one being "very little" and ten being "a great deal"), rate how much "doing" you do in relation to wealth building.

1——2——3——4——5——6——7——8——9——10

15. Wattles encourages you to lay aside all other books on manifesting abundance until you master these concepts,

claiming that you need not learn any more than the contents of this book. Do you think you could stop searching for the answer after reading this book and practicing the exercises in this manual? Make a commitment to do so. Make a note of any feelings that arise in response to making this commitment.

16. Wattles instructs you to "Read this book every day; keep it with you; commit it to memory, and do not think about others "systems" and theories." Doing so will only create doubts, and will ultimately cause you to fail. Other experts suggest that you surround yourself with self-help audios, books, affirmations, etc. Which suggestion would you follow and why do you choose to do so?

17. Wattles also encourages you to stay away from studying the occult, religions or other such studies. Doing so creates mental crosscurrents, which will bring your hopes to shipwreck. Do you currently study the occult or religions that may interfere with manifesting riches? If so, could you give up these studies while you follow your journey towards abundance?

18. "There is a thinking stuff from which all things are made, and which, in its original state, permeates, penetrates, and fills the interspaces of the universe." If this thinking stuff fills the interspaces of the universe, how might you create more space in your life to allow the thinking stuff to penetrate your world? Is your life physically and mentally cluttered? How might you be able to clear more space?

Chapter 11

Acting In The Certain Way

Thought is the creative power, or the impelling force which causes the creative power to act; thinking in a Certain Way will bring riches to you, but you must not rely upon thought alone, paying no attention to personal action. That is the rock upon which many otherwise scientific metaphysical thinkers meet shipwreck—the failure to connect thought with personal action. We have not yet reached the stage of development, even supposing such a stage to be possible, in which man can create directly from Formless Substance without nature's processes or the work of human hands; man must not only think, but his personal action must supplement his thought. By thought you can cause the gold in the hearts of the mountains to be impelled toward you; but it will not mine itself, refine itself, coin itself into double eagles, and come rolling along the roads seeking its way into your pocket.

Under the impelling power of the Supreme Spirit, men's affairs will be so ordered that some one will be led to mine the gold for you; other men's business transactions will be so directed that the gold will be brought toward you, and you must so arrange your own business affairs that you may be able to receive it when it comes to you. Your thought makes all things, animate and inanimate, work to bring you what you want; but your personal activity must be such that you can rightly receive what you want when it reaches you. You are not to take it as charity, nor to steal it; you must give every man more in use value than he gives you in cash value.

The scientific use of thought consists in forming a clear and distinct mental image of what you want; in holding fast to the purpose to get what you want; and in realizing with grateful faith that you do get what you want. Do not try to 'project' your thought in any mysterious or occult way, with the idea of having it go out and do things for you; that is wasted effort, and will weaken your power to think with sanity. The action of thought in getting rich is fully explained in the preceding chapters; your faith and purpose positively impress your vision upon Formless Substance, which has THE SAME DESIRE FOR MORE LIFE THAT YOU HAVE; and this vision, received from you, sets all the creative forces at work IN AND THROUGH THEIR REGULAR CHANNELS OF ACTION, but directed toward you. It is not your part to guide or supervise the creative process; all you have to do with that is to retain your vision, stick to your purpose, and maintain your faith and gratitude.

But you must act in a Certain Way, so that you can appropriate what is yours when it comes to you; so that you can meet the things you have in your picture, and put them in their proper places as they arrive. You can really see the truth of this. When things reach you, they will be in the hands of other men, who will ask an equivalent for them. And you can only get what is yours by giving the other man what is his. Your pocketbook is not going to be transformed into a Fortunata's purse, which shall be always full of money without effort on your part. This is the crucial point in the science of getting rich; right here, where thought and personal action must be combined. There are very many people who, consciously or unconsciously, set the creative forces in action by the strength and persistence of their desires, but who remain poor because they do not provide for the reception of the thing they want when it comes. By thought, the thing you want is brought to you; by action you receive it.

Whatever your action is to be, it is evident that you must act NOW. You cannot act in the past, and it is essential to the clearness of your mental vision that you dismiss the past from your mind. You cannot act in the future, for the future is not here yet. And you cannot tell how you will want to act in any future contingency until that contingency has arrived. Because you are not in the right business, or the right environment now, do not think that you must postpone action until you get into the right business or environment. And do not spend time in the present taking thought as to the best course in possible future emergencies; have faith in your ability to meet any emergency when it arrives.

If you act in the present with your mind on the future, your present action will be with a divided mind, and will not be effective. Put your whole mind into present action. Do not give your creative impulse to Original Substance, and then sit down and wait for results; if you do, you will never get them. Act now. There is never any time but now, and there never will be any time but now. If you are ever to begin to make ready for the reception of what you want, you must begin now. And your action, whatever it is, must most likely be in your present business or employment, and must be upon the persons and things in your present environment.

You cannot act where you are not; you cannot act where you have been, and you cannot act where you are going to be; you can act only where you are. Do not bother as to whether yesterday's work was well done or ill done; do to-day's work well.

Do not try to do tomorrow's work now; there will be plenty of time to do that when you get to it. Do not try, by occult or mystical means, to act on people or things that are out of your reach. Do not wait for a change of environment, before you act; get a change of environment by action. You can so act upon the environment in which you are now, as to cause yourself to be transferred to a better environment. Hold with faith and purpose the vision of yourself in the better environment, but act upon your present environment with all your heart, and with all your strength, and with all your mind. Do not spend any time in day dreaming or castle building; hold to the one vision of what you want, and act NOW.

Do not cast about seeking some new thing to do, or some strange, unusual, or remarkable action to perform as a first step toward getting rich. It is probable that your actions, at least for some time to come, will be those you have been performing for some time past; but you are to begin now to perform these actions in the Certain Way, which will surely make you rich. If you are engaged in some business, and feel that it is not the right one for you, do not wait until you get into the right business before you begin to act.

Do not feel discouraged, or sit down and lament because you are misplaced. No man was ever so misplaced but that he could not find the right place, and no man ever became so involved in the wrong business but that he could get into the right business. Hold the vision of yourself in the right business, with the purpose to get into it, and the faith that you will get into it, and are getting into it; but ACT in your present business. Use your present business as the means of getting a better one, and use your present environment as the means of getting into a better one. Your vision of the right business, if held with faith and purpose, will cause the Supreme to move the right business toward you; and your action, if performed in the Certain Way, will cause you to move toward the business.

If you are an employee, or wage earner, and feel that you must change places in order to get what you want, do not 'project" your thought into space and rely upon it to get you another job. It will probably fail to do so. Hold the vision of yourself in the job you want, while you ACT with faith and purpose on the job you have, and you will certainly get the job you want. Your vision and faith will set the creative force in motion to bring it toward you, and your action will cause the forces in your own environment to move you toward the place you want. In closing this chapter, we will add another statement to our syllabus:

There is a thinking stuff from which all things are made, and which, in its original state, permeates, penetrates, and fills the interspaces of the universe. A thought, in this substance, Produces the thing that is imaged by the thought. Man can form things in his thought, and, by impressing his thought upon formless substance, can cause the thing he thinks about to be created. In order to do this, man must pass from the competitive to the creative mind; he must form a clear mental picture of the things he wants, and hold this picture in his thoughts with the fixed PURPOSE to get what he wants, and the unwavering FAITH that he does get what he wants, closing his mind to all that may tend to shake his purpose, dim his vision, or quench his faith. That he may receive what he wants when it comes, man must act NOW upon the people and things in his present environment.

Acting In The Certain Way

1. Wattles opens this chapter with a caution not to rely on thoughts alone, but to connect thought with personal action in order to bring riches to you. He likens your thoughts to gold that cannot mine itself, and needs your actions to mine it. Have you taken any definitive actions yet towards manifesting the abundance that you desire in your life? If so, what are they?

2. "Men's affairs will be so ordered that someone will be led to mine the gold for you; other men's business trans-actions will be so directed that the gold will be brought toward you." Wattles asserts that you must arrange your own business affairs so that you may be able to receive the gold that comes to you when it does. How do you feel when you learn that others will be led to you and that they will bring the gold towards you?

3. Reflect on your inner thoughts and feelings. Have you had difficulty receiving from others in the past? If so, list who you struggled with and why.

4. Are you now willing and ready to receive abundance in your life? What has changed and what evidence do you have of that change?

5. There is a fine line between having your thoughts, and absolutely believing them, as opposed to trying to project

them into becoming. Wattles warns to not "project" your thought in any mysterious or occult ways, with the idea to have it go out and do things for you. Have you been trying to project your thoughts into manifesting, as opposed to trusting that they will?

6. It is not your responsibility to guide or supervise the creative process. All you need to do is retain your vision, stick to your purpose and maintain your faith and gratitude. When we have fear, we often consciously or unconsciously try to control our lives. How much do you try to control your life? On a scale from one to ten (one being "very little" and ten being "a great deal"), rate how much you attempt to control all aspects of your life.

7. Do you, in any way try to control the creative process in your life? If so, how?

8. The author asserts that you will be able to see the truth of the fact that when things reach you, they will be in the hands of others. Start paying attention and setting an intent to have this truth revealed to you. When it is, whether big or small, write about it in a journal or diary. Doing so sets your attention on such circumstances and enhances your ability to manifest.

9. You are now at the crucial part of *The Science of Getting Rich*—where thought and personal action must be combined. You must act "now" and not in the past or future. How much time do you spend reviewing your past? On a scale from one to ten (one being "very little" and ten being "a great deal"), rate how much time you do so.

1——2——3——4——5——6——7——8——9——10

10. How much time do you spend projecting into the future? On a scale from one to ten (one being "very little" and ten being "a great deal"), rate how much time you do so.

11. How much time do you spend living in the present moment? On a scale from one to ten (one being "very little" and ten being "a great deal"), rate how much time you do so.

12. Wattles emphasizes that you must not postpone action until you get into the right business or environment. Be honest with yourself. Have you been waiting for "better conditions" to arrive in your life, before you take action towards manifesting abundance? Write about the beliefs that you have around postponing your dreams.

13. Again, being truly honest with yourself, have you been setting your beliefs on "someday in the future" for attaining wealth? If so, note when you do so, and think "cancel" to remind yourself that you are thinking as such, and to cancel the energy that you have projected.

14. Your immediate action must be in your present business or employment, and must be upon the persons and things in your present environment. When you are acting "in a Certain Way", notice the impulses that come to you in the present moment. Observe how they feel versus wishing that you had taken action yesterday, or hoping that you'll get another opportunity to act tomorrow. Write about any insights you gain while doing this exercise.

15. Wattles says that you can start by doing today's work well. He states, "you can act upon the environment in

which you are now, as to cause yourself to be transferred to a better environment." Are you giving your most in your current employment situation?

16. How might you imagine your current work environment changing for the better?

17. To do a recap, have you moved from competitive mind to creative? Do you have a clear mental picture of what you desire? Do you have a fixed purpose to get what you want and unwavering faith that it will come to be? Have you closed your mind to everything that could shake you from your purpose, dim your vision or squelch your faith? Are you acting NOW upon the people and situations at your present place of employment? If you have not answered "yes" to each of the above questions, then review and practice the previous exercises in this manual so that you are creating a free and clear path towards manifesting abundance in your life.

Chapter 12

Efficient Action

You must use your thought as directed in previous chapters, and begin to do what you can do where you are; and you must do ALL that you can do where you are. You can advance only be being larger than your present place; and no man is larger than his present place who leaves undone any of the work pertaining to that place.

The world is advanced only by those who more than fill their present places. If no man quite filled his present place, you can see that there must be a going backward in everything. Those who do not quite fill their present places are dead weight upon society, government, commerce, and industry; they must be carried along by others at a great expense. The progress of the world is retarded only by those who do not fill the places they are holding; they belong to a former age and a lower stage or plane of life, and their tendency is toward degeneration. No society could advance if every man was smaller than his place; social evolution is guided by the law of physical and mental evolution. In the animal world, evolution is caused by excess of life. When an organism has more life than can be expressed in the functions of its own plane, it develops the organs of a higher plane, and a new species is originated.

There never would have been new species had there not been organisms which more than filled their places. The law is exactly the same for you; your getting rich depends upon your applying this principle to your own affairs. Every day is either a successful day or a day of failure; and it is the successful days which get you what you want. If everyday is a failure, you can never get rich; while if every day is a success, you cannot fail to get rich. If there is something that may be done today, and you do not do it, you have failed in so far as that thing is concerned; and the consequences may be more disastrous than you imagine.

You cannot foresee the results of even the most trivial act; you do not know the workings of all the forces that have been set moving in your behalf. Much may be depending on your doing some simple act; it may be the very thing which is to open the door of opportunity to very great possibilities. You can never know all the combinations which Supreme Intelligence is making for you in the world of things and of things and of human affairs; your neglect or failure to do some small thing may cause a long delay in getting what you want.

Do, every day, ALL that can be done that day. There is, however, a limitation or qualification of the above that you must take into account. You are not to overwork, nor to rush blindly into your business in the effort to do the greatest possible number of things in the shortest possible time.

You are not to try to do tomorrow's work today, nor to do a week's work in a day. It is really not the number of things you do, but the EFFICIENCY of each separate action that counts. Every act is, in itself, either a success or a failure.

Every act is, in itself, either effective or inefficient.
Every inefficient act is a failure, and if you spend your life in doing inefficient acts, your whole life will be a failure.
The more things you do, the worse for you, if all your acts are inefficient ones.

On the other hand, every efficient act is a success in itself, and if every act of your life is an efficient one, your whole life MUST be a success. The cause of failure is doing too many things in an inefficient manner, and not doing enough things in an efficient manner. You will see that it is a self-evident proposition that if you do not do any inefficient acts, and if you do a sufficient number of efficient acts, you will become rich. If, now, it is possible for you to make each act an efficient one, you see again that the getting of riches is reduced to an exact science, like mathematics.

The matter turns, then, on the questions whether you can make each separate act a success in itself. And this you can certainly do. You can make each act a success, because ALL Power is working with you; and ALL Power cannot fail. Power is at your service; and to make each act efficient you have only to put power into it. Every action is either strong or weak; and when every one is strong, you are acting in the Certain Way which will make you rich. Every act can be made strong and efficient by holding your vision while you are doing it, and putting the whole power of your FAITH and PURPOSE into it.

It is at this point that the people fail who separate mental power from personal action. They use the power of mind in one place and at one time, and they act in another pace and at another time. So their acts are not successful in themselves; too many of them are inefficient. But if ALL Power goes into every act, no matter how commonplace, every act will be a success in itself; and as in the nature of things every success opens the way to other successes, your progress toward what you want, and the progress of what you want toward you, will become increasingly rapid.

Remember that successful action is cumulative in its results. Since the desire for more life is inherent in all things, when a man begins to move toward larger life more things attach themselves to him, and the influence of his desire is multiplied. Do, every day, all that you can do that day, and do each act in an efficient manner. In saying that you must hold your vision while you are doing each act, however trivial or commonplace, I do not mean to say that it is necessary at all times to see the vision distinctly to its smallest details. It should be the work of your leisure hours to use your imagination on the details of your vision, and to contemplate them until they are firmly fixed upon memory. If you wish speedy results, spend practically all your spare time in this practice. By continuous contemplation you will get the picture of what you want, even to the smallest details, so firmly fixed upon your mind, and so completely transferred to the mind of Formless Substance, that in your working hours you need only to mentally refer to the picture to stimulate your faith and purpose, and cause your best effort to be put forth. Contemplate your picture in your leisure hours until your consciousness is so full of it that you can grasp it instantly. You will become so enthused with its bright promises that the mere thought of it will call forth the strongest energies of your whole being.

Let us again repeat our syllabus, and by slightly changing the closing statements bring it to the point we have now reached. There is a thinking stuff from which all things are made, and which, in its original state, permeates, penetrates, and fills the interspaces of the universe. A thought, in this substance, Produces the thing that is imaged by the thought. Man can form things in his thought, and, by impressing his thought upon formless substance, can cause the thing he thinks about to be created. In order to do this, man must pass from the competitive to the creative mind; he must form a clear mental picture of the things he wants, and do, with faith and purpose, all that can be done each day, doing each separate thing in an efficient manner.

STUDY GUIDE

Efficient Action

1. Wattles states that "The world is advanced only by those who more than fill their present places." He says that you can only advance by being larger than your present place. Are you doing all that you can in your present state to be "larger," leaving no task undone? How might you improve upon your current work performance?

2. According to the author, the progress of the world is retarded only by those who do not fill the places that they are holding. Reflect on all aspects of your life: your friendships, family relationships, career endeavors, personal endeavors, creative expressions, areas of study, methods of self-care, etc. Do an inventory. Make a list of the areas in which you are not fully living your best in each area of your life.

3. In each of the areas you feel that you could improve upon, make a list of action steps you can now take to better yourself and your performance.

4. Regarding the evolution of life, Wattles states, "There never would have been new species had there not been organisms which more than filled their places." Your getting rich depends upon applying this principle to your own life. Are you ready to emerge as the new you? What changes do you see in yourself? Visualize and then describe them in as much detail as possible.

5. The successful days that you have in your life give you what you want. Focus on the next seven days in your life. At the end of each day, ask yourself whether you felt your day was a success. Track each day in the listing below. Do the successes outnumber the failures?

	Failure	Success
Day 1	_____	_____
Day 2	_____	_____
Day 3	_____	_____
Day 4	_____	_____
Day 5	_____	_____
Day 6	_____	_____
Day 7	_____	_____

6. According to Wattles, the consequences for failing to do something that may need to be done today may be more disastrous than you might imagine. It could cause a long delay in getting what you want. Write about a situation where you neglected to do something, big or small, and that neglect caused major consequences for you.

7. Finding balance between doing all that you can do in a day, yet not overworking, can be a challenge. What are you currently doing to maintain balance in your life?

8. "It is really not the number of things you do, but the EFFICIENCY of each separate action that counts." Are you efficient at the tasks that you accomplish? How so? If not, how might you become more efficient?

9. Failure can be the result of doing too many things in an inefficient manner, and not doing enough things in an

efficient manner. Do you have a tendency to fall short in either of the two behaviors?

10. Success lies in making each separate act a success in itself. Are you steadfast in trying to do all that you do well? Are there any areas where you feel you fall short in your life? If so, describe them.

11. Wattles states that power is at your service. Do you have a tendency not to trust this as being so? If so, do you exhaust yourself through overdoing things, believing that you and you alone create your reality? Write about your beliefs and habits around over-exertion.

12. On a scale from one to ten (one being "very little" and ten being "a great deal"), rate how fatigued you find yourself at the end of each day.

1——2——3——4——5——6——7——8——9——10

13. Do you sometimes try to push "weak" actions, instead of focusing on putting your faith and purpose into strong ones?

14. For the next month, focus your energy on only those actions that feel strong. Do not move forward on actions that feel weak. This may be difficult in the beginning because you are breaking old, ingrained habits, but keep committed and focused on this exercise. Note any changes as you do so.

15. After the month, go back to the scale in #12 and rate your energy at the end of the day. In general do you find that you have more energy? If not, continue with the exercise in #14 for an additional month. Write about your progress.

16. The author states that every success opens the way to other successes. Write about an experience where you

see this to be so. Try to find something in your life that supports this truth. If not, find one from someone else's life that will.

17. "When a man beings to move toward larger life more things attach themselves to him, and the influence of his desire is multiplied." Are you moving toward a larger life? If so, how has the influence of your desire multiplied? If not, in your mind's eye, imagine it multiplying. What do you see, smell, taste, hear and feel? Write about your experience.

18. Wattles suggests that you spend practically all of your spare time contemplating what you want if you desire speedy results. How much of your spare time do you spend contemplating what you would like to manifest in your life?

19. Could you commit to spending more time contemplating them? If so, how much more time each day could you commit to?

20. Does getting a mental picture of what you want instill instant energy of your whole being? If so, write about how you feel when you contemplate it. If not, spend more of your leisure time contemplating and feeling into your desires.

21. Have you noted any additional manifestations when you contemplate your desires? Are you experiencing any stronger images, sounds, smells or feelings? Take a few minutes to write out that which you wish to manifest in your life. Again, write about it in as much sensory detail as possible. Then compare it with your earlier accounts. Has it changed in any way?

Chapter 13

Getting Into The Right Business

Success, in any particular business, depends for one thing upon your possessing in a well-developed state the faculties required in that business. Without good musical faculty no one can succeed as a teacher of music; without well-developed mechanical faculties no one can achieve great success in any of the mechanical trades; without tact and the commercial faculties no one can succeed in mercantile pursuits. But to possess in a well developed state the faculties required in your particular vocation does not insure getting rich. There are musicians who have remarkable talent, and who yet remain poor; there are blacksmiths, carpenters, and so on who have excellent mechanical ability, but who do not get rich; and there are merchants with good faculties for dealing with men who nevertheless fail. The different faculties are tools; it is essential to have good tools, but it is also essential that the tools should be used in the Right Way. One man can take a sharp saw, a square, a good plane, and so on, and build a handsome article of furniture;

another man can take the same tools and set to work to duplicate the article, but his production will be a botch. He does not know how to use good tools in a successful way.

The various faculties of your mind are the tools with which you must do the work which is to make you rich; it will be easier for you to succeed if you get into a business for which you are well equipped with mental tools. Generally speaking, you will do best in that business which will use your strongest faculties; the one for which you are naturally "best fitted." But there are limitations to this statement, also. No man should regard his vocation as being irrevocably fixed by the tendencies with which he was born. You can get rich in ANY business, for if you have not the right talent for you can develop that talent; it merely means that you will have to make your tools as you go along, instead of confining yourself to the use of those with which you were born. It will be EASIER for you to succeed in a vocation for which you already have the talents in a well-developed state; but you CAN succeed in any vocation, for you can develop any rudimentary talent, and there is no talent of which you have not at least the rudiment. You will get rich most easily in point of effort, if you do that for which you are best fitted; but you will get rich most satisfactorily if you do that which you WANT to do.

Doing what you want to do is life; and there is no real satisfaction in living if we are compelled to be forever doing something which we do not like to do, and can never do what we want to do. And it is certain that you can do what you want to do; the desire to do it is proof that you have within you the power which can do it.

Desire is a manifestation of power. The desire to play music is the power which can play music seeking expression and development; the desire to invent mechanical devices is the mechanical talent seeking expression and development. Where there is no power, either developed or undeveloped, to do a thing, there is never any desire to do that thing; and where there is strong desire to do a thing, it is certain proof that the power to do it is strong, and only requires to be developed and applied in the Right Way. All things else being equal, it is best to select the business for which you have the best developed talent; but if you have a strong desire to engage in any particular line of work, you should select that work as the ultimate end at which you aim.

You can do what you want to do, and it is your right and privilege to follow the business or avocation which will be most congenial and pleasant. You are not obliged to do what you do not like to do, and should not do it except as a means to bring you to the doing of the thing you want to do. If there are past mistakes whose consequences have placed you in an undesirable business or environment, you may be obliged for some time to do what you do not like to do; but you can make the doing of it pleasant by knowing that it is making it possible for you to come to the doing of what you want to do.

If you feel that you are not in the right vocation, do not act too hastily in trying to get into another one. The best way, generally, to change business or environment is by growth. Do not be afraid to make a sudden and radical change if the opportunity is presented, and you feel after careful consideration that it is the right opportunity; but never take sudden or radical action when you are in doubt as to the wisdom of doing so.

There is never any hurry on the creative plane; and there is no lack of opportunity. When you get out of the competitive mind you will understand that you never need to act hastily. No one else is going to beat you to the thing you want to do; there is enough for all. If one space is taken, another and a better one will be opened for you a little farther on; there is plenty of time. When you are in doubt, wait. Fall back on the contemplation of your vision, and increase your faith and purpose; and by all means, in times of doubt and indecision, cultivate gratitude.

A day or two spent in contemplating the vision of what you want, and in earnest thanksgiving that you are getting it, will bring your mind into such close relationship with the Supreme that you will make no mistake when you do act. There is a mind which knows all there is to know; and you can come into close unity with this mind by faith and the purpose to advance in life, if you have deep gratitude.

Mistakes come from acting hastily, or from acting in fear or doubt, or in forgetfulness of the Right Motive, which is more life to all, and less to none. As you go on in the Certain Way, opportunities will come to you in increasing number; and you will need to be very steady in your faith and purpose, and to keep in close touch with the All Mind by reverent gratitude. Do all that you can do in a perfect manner every day, but do it without haste, worry, or fear. Go as fast as you can, but never hurry. Remember that in the moment you begin to hurry you cease to be a creator and become a competitor; you drop back upon the old plane again.

Whenever you find yourself hurrying, call a halt; fix your attention on the mental image of the thing you want, and begin to give thanks that you are getting it. The exercise of GRATITUDE will never fail to strengthen your faith and renew your purpose.

STUDY GUIDE

Getting Into the Right Business

1. Wattles opens this chapter stating that it is easier to get rich with a business that utilizes the talents you were born with, rather than trying to cultivate new talents. Make a list of all of your talents.

2. Go through the list you created in #1, and mark each with whether you are average or above average in each talent.

3. Make a list of the talents that you believe you need to succeed in your business desires.

4. Go through the lists you created in #1 and #3. Do your talents match the skills required to successfully succeed in your business desires?

5. Based on your previous inquiry, create a list of the talents that you need to further cultivate in order to create your desired success. What action steps can you take to further train yourself in these areas of expertise?

6. Wallace Wattles states, "You will get rich most easily if you do that for which you are best fitted; but you will get rich most satisfactorily if you do that which you WANT to do." Do your current desires integrate what you are good at with what you wish to do? How so? If not, what is missing from the scenario? Are there any actions that you can take to successfully meld your competencies with your desires?

7. If your desire is a manifestation of your power, then it is proof that you have the power to manifest it. Take some time to investigate whether or not you are under-estimating your power. List ways in which you are doing so.

8. What can you do empower yourself further, especially in relation to manifesting your dreams?

9. Wattles encourages you not to act hastily if you feel you are in the wrong vocation; however, he suggests you make changes if the opportunity presents itself. Reflect on your current vocation. Have you missed any opportunities to move into something more suited to your taste? If so, did you sabotage yourself in any way by not making the move? If not, pay attention to anything that might be a sign for movement.

10. There is never any hurry or lack of opportunity in the creative plane. Do you believe this, or do you often find yourself anxiously feeling a sense of urgency with regards to "doing" so that you can get where you really want to go?

11. If you have this sense of urgency, do you feel it supports your journey towards achieving your dreams? How so?

12. When in doubt, Wattles encourages you to spend additional time contemplating the vision of what you want while feeling grateful that it is coming to you. Take some time to do this exercise now, and write about your experience and any insights that you may have gained.

13. Mistakes come from acting hastily through fear and doubt. When have you acted hastily with life decisions and how has doing so backfired on you?

14. Creating hurry drops you back down into competitive mode again. Pay attention throughout the next week to

times when you feel urgency and anxiousness. How do these feelings affect your overall energy?

15. Halting on hurrying, fixing a mental image of what you want, and appreciating your receiving it strengthens your faith and renews your purpose. Wattles says that in doing so, you will never fail. Take 10 minutes to focus on all that you desire. See and feel it coming to you, and fill your heart with gratitude for the co-creation of it all.

16. Write a poem, prayer or statement of gratitude for the gifts that are awaiting you. Allow yourself to fully express your gratitude in imaginative and creative ways. You may also wish to collage, paint or draw. Feel free to fully express your gratitude on whatever way you feel inclined.

Chapter 14

The Impression Of Increase

Whether you change your vocation or not, your actions for the present must be those pertaining to the business in which you are now engaged. You can get into the business you want by making constructive use of the business you are already established in; by doing your daily work in a Certain Way.

And in so far as your business consists in dealing with other men, whether personally or by letter, the key-thought of all your efforts must be to convey to their minds the impression of increase. Increase is what all men and all women are seeking; it is the urge of the Formless Intelligence within them, seeking fuller expression. The desire for increase is inherent in all nature; it is the fundamental impulse of the universe. All human activities are based on the desire for increase; people are seeking more food, more clothes, better shelter, more luxury, more beauty, more knowledge, more pleasure—increase in something, more life.

Every living thing is under this necessity for continuous advancement; where increase of life ceases, dissolution and death set in at once. Man instinctively knows this, and hence he is forever seeking more. This law of perpetual increase is set forth by Jesus in the parable of the talents; only those who gain more retain any; from him who hath not shall be taken away even that which he hath. The normal desire for increased wealth is not an evil or a reprehensible thing; it is simply the desire for more abundant life; it is aspiration. And because it is the deepest instinct of their natures, all men and women are attracted to him who can give them more of the means of life. In following the Certain Way as described in the foregoing pages, you are getting continuous increase for yourself, and you are giving it to all with whom you deal.

You are a creative center, from which increase is given off to all. Be sure of this, and convey assurance of the fact to every man, woman, and child with whom you come in contact. No matter how small the transaction, even if it be only the selling of a stick of candy to a little child, put into it the thought of increase, and make sure that the customer is impressed with the thought. Convey the impression of advancement with everything you do, so that all people shall receive the impression that you are an Advancing Man, and that you advance all who deal with you. Even to the people whom you meet in a social way, without any thought of business, and to whom you do not try to sell anything, give the thought of increase.

You can convey this impression by holding the unshakable faith that you, yourself, are in the Way of

Increase; and by letting this faith inspire, fill, and permeate every action. Do everything that you do in the firm conviction that you are an advancing personality, and that you are giving advancement to everybody. Feel that you are getting rich, and that in so doing you are making others rich, and conferring benefits on all.

Do not boast or brag of your success, or talk about it unnecessarily; true faith is never boastful. Wherever you find a boastful person, you find one who is secretly doubtful and afraid. Simply feel the faith, and let it work out in every transaction; let every act and tone and look express the quiet assurance that you are getting rich; that you are already rich. Words will not be necessary to communicate this feeling to others; they will feel the sense of increase when in your presence, and will be attracted to you again. You must so impress others that they will feel that in associating with you they will get increase for themselves. See that you give them a use value greater than the cash value you are taking from them.

Take an honest pride in doing this, and let everybody know it; and you will have no lack of customers. People will go where they are given increase; and the Supreme, which desires increase in all, and which knows all, will move toward you men and women who have never heard of you. Your business will increase rapidly, and you will be surprised at the unexpected benefits which will come to you. You will be able from day to day to make larger combinations, secure greater advantages, and to go on into a more congenial vocation if you desire to do so. But doing thing all this, you must never lose sight of your vision of what you want, or your faith and purpose to get what you want. Let me here give you another word of caution in regard to motives.

Beware of the insidious temptation to seek for power over other men. Nothing is so pleasant to the unformed or partially developed mind as the exercise of power or dominion over others. The desire to rule for selfish gratification has been the curse of the world. For countless ages kings and lords have drenched the earth with blood in their battles to extend their dominions; this not to seek more life for all, but to get more power for themselves.

To-day, the main motive in the business and industrial world is the same; men Marshal their armies of dollars, and lay waste the lives and hearts of millions in the same mad scramble for power over others. Commercial kings, like political kings, are inspired by the lust for power.

Jesus saw in this desire for mastery the moving impulse of that evil world He sought to overthrow. Read the twenty-third chapter of Matthew, and see how He pictures the lust of the Pharisees to be called "Master," to sit in the high places, to domineer over others, and to lay burdens on the backs of the less fortunate; and note how He compares this lust for dominion with the brotherly seeking for the Common Good to which He calls His disciples. Look out for the temptation to seek for authority, to become a "master," to be considered as one who is above the common herd, to impress others by lavish display, and so on. The mind that seeks for mastery over others is the competitive mind; and the competitive mind is not the creative one. In order to master your environment and your destiny, it is not at all necessary that you should rule over your fellow men and indeed, when you fall into the world's struggle for the high places, you begin to be conquered by fate and environment, and your getting rich becomes a matter of chance and speculation. Beware of the competitive mind!! No better statement of the principle of creative action can be formulated than the favorite declaration of the late "Golden Rule" Jones of Toledo: "What I want for myself, I want for everybody."

STUDY GUIDE

The Impression of Increase

1. You can work on your future business by doing your current business's daily work in a Certain Way. The key thought of all your efforts must be "to convey to their minds the impression of increase". Contemplate your current position and those with whom you work. Write a list of those you come in contact with on a regular basis— your co-workers, vendors, clients and anyone else in your work environment.

2. Now with each, list ways in which you can convey the impression of increase to them. Write down at least two concrete actions that you can take with each individual.

3. Make the verbal commitment to yourself aloud, that hereon in you will convey increase to all you meet during your workday.

4. Wattles explains that because the desire for increase is the deepest instinct of one's nature, all are attracted to those who can give them more of the means of life. Now take a look at your personal life. Make a list of your friends, family members and others you come in contact with.

5. How can you convey the impression of increase to each of the individuals on your "personal" list? Write at least two to three actions that you can take to do so and begin to take immediate action.

6. Write about any insights you gain by following through on conveying increases to those around you. How did your decision affect others? How did it affect you?

7. Did you notice any differences in your energy or in others you touched by conveying increase? If so, write about what you noted.

8. Once you commit to conveying increase, you become "a creative center, from which increase is given off to all". Take a moment to visualize yourself as that creative center. See abundant energy radiating to you and through you to others. Feel into this radiance now and know that it is so.

9. Next time you feel low in energy, imagine yourself as that golden center of creative radiance funneling abundant increase to all around you (including you). See yourself filled with creative energy. Note any shift in your energy after doing this exercise.

10. Wattles encourages you to put the impression of advancement into every transaction that you encounter— from small to large. He gives the example of selling a stick of candy to a little child. Take note of the short or simple encounters you have with others. How are you conveying increase in these transactions? Share at least five such transactions you have during the next week. Write about them and how you conveyed advancement in those situations.

11. List at least three things that you do or say to give others the impression that you are an Advancing Man or Woman.

12. Wattles insists that true faith is never boastful. In fact, it shows that you are secretly doubtful and afraid. Let's explore your boastfulness. List when and with whom you

catch yourself boasting. Do you ever do so at work? Do you do so among friends? Do you boast when you are doing business networking? Do you do it when you are socializing? Do you do it with the opposite sex, or with colleagues?

13. Check in after you boast. How do you feel? Do you feel your energy has increased or decreased after the exchange?

14. Reflect on the last time you boasted. How might you have handled the situation better, in a way that encouraged and empowered you and those you were engaged with?

15. Wattles states, "See that you give them (others) a use value greater than the cash value you are taking from them". Think of the last time you took cash from someone. Did you give them greater value than the cash they gave you in the exchange? How?

16. According to the author, when you give greater value, the Supreme will move men and women towards you who have never heard of you. Reflect on your past. Was there a time when individuals appeared in your life and were vital in moving you forward in a direction you wanted to go? If so, how were you radiating abundance and giving more in your life?

17. If you can't think of a situation where someone unexpectedly appeared and assisted you in your advancement, make a commitment to take note when such circumstances arise. Expect them to happen, have faith; follow the tenets of this book and express gratitude for their outcome. Write about your experience once it manifests in your life.

18. Wattles cautions you about seeking power over others. "The desire to rule for selfish gratification has been the curse of the world." How have you sought power in your life?

19. What was the outcome when you tried to seek power?

20. How did you feel about yourself when you sought power? Did you feel authentically empowered? Was something amiss? If so, what?

21. List three individuals who you believe have sought power for selfish gratification.

22. List three individuals who became powerful through authentic commitment to goodness and growth.

23. Do you have a tendency to want to be a "master" over others? Be very honest with yourself and lists ways in which you believe you are "above" others.'

24. How does believing you are "better than" serve you? How does it serve others?

25. Jones of Toledo declared, "What I want for myself, I want for everybody." Do you really want all you have for everyone else as well? If you find that you have any blocks in extending your desires to others for manifestation, write about them and find a way to make peace with them within your heart.

Chapter 15

The Advancing Man

What I have said in the last chapter applies as well to the professional man and the wage-earner as to the man who is engaged in mercantile business. No matter whether you are a physician, a teacher, or a clergyman, if you can give increase of life to others and make them sensible of the fact, they will be attracted to you, and you will get rich. The physician who holds the vision of himself as a great and successful healer, and who works toward the complete realization of that vision with faith and purpose, as described in former chapters, will come into such close touch with the Source of Life that he will be phenomenally successful; patients will come to him in throngs. No one has a greater opportunity to carry into effect the teaching of this book than the practitioner of medicine; it does not matter to which of the various schools he may belong, for the principle of healing is common to all of them, and may be reached by all alike. The Advancing Man in medicine, who holds to a clear mental image of himself as successful, and who obeys the laws of faith, purpose, and gratitude, will cure every curable case he undertakes, no matter what remedies he may use. In the field of religion, the world cries out for the clergyman who can teach his hearers the true science of abundant life. He who masters the details of the science of getting rich, together with the allied sciences of being well, of being great, and of winning love, and who teaches these details from the pulpit, will never lack for a congregation. This is the gospel that the world needs; it will give increase of life, and men will hear it gladly, and will give liberal support to the man who brings it to them.

What is now needed is a demonstration of the science of life from the pulpit. We want preachers who can not only tell us how, but who in their own persons will show us how. We need the preacher who will himself be rich, healthy, great, and beloved, to teach us how to attain to these things; and when he comes he will find a numerous and loyal following. The same is true of the teacher who can inspire the children with the faith and purpose of the advancing life. He will never be "out of a job." And any teacher who has this faith and purpose can give it to his pupils; he cannot help giving it to them if it is part of his own life and practice. What is true of the teacher, preacher, and physician is true of the lawyer, dentist, real estate man, insurance agent—of everybody.

The combined mental and personal action I have described is infallible; it cannot fail. Every man and woman who follows these instructions steadily, perseveringly, and to the letter, will get rich. The law of the

Increase of Life is as mathematically certain in its operation as the law of gravitation; getting rich is an exact science.

The wage-earner will find this as true of his case as of any of the others mentioned. Do not feel that you have no chance to get rich because you are working where there is no visible opportunity for advancement, where wages are small and the cost of living high. Form your clear mental vision of what you want, and begin to act with faith and purpose. Do all the work you can do, every day, and do each piece of work in a perfectly successful manner; put the power of success, and the purpose to get rich, into everything that you do.

But do not do this merely with the idea of currying favor with your employer, in the hope that he, or those above you, will see your good work and advance you; it is not likely that they will do so. The man who is merely a "good" workman, filling his place to the very best of his ability, and satisfied with that, is valuable to his employer; and it is not to the employer's interest to promote him; he is worth more where he is.

To secure advancement, something more is necessary than to be too large for your place. The man who is certain to advance is the one who is too big for his place, and who has a clear concept of what he wants to be; who knows that he can become what he wants to be and who is determined to BE what he wants to be. Do not try to more than fill your present place with a view to pleasing your employer; do it with the idea of advancing yourself. Hold the faith and purpose of increase during work hours, after work hours, and before work hours. Hold it in such a way that every person who comes in contact with you, whether foreman, fellow workman, or social acquaintance, will feel the power of purpose radiating from you; so that every one will get the sense of advancement and increase from you. Men will be attracted to you, and if there is no possibility for advancement in your present job, you will very soon see an opportunity to take another job.

There is a Power which never fails to present opportunity to the Advancing Man who is moving in obedience to law. God cannot help helping you, if you act in a Certain Way; He must do so in order to help Himself. There is nothing in your circumstances or in the industrial situation that can keep you down. If you cannot get rich working for the steel trust, you can get rich on a ten-acre farm; and if you begin to move in the Certain Way, you will certainly escape from the "clutches" of the steel trust and get on to the farm or wherever else you wish to be.

If a few thousands of its employees would enter upon the Certain Way, the steel trust would soon be in a bad plight; it would have to give its workingmen more opportunity, or go out of business. Nobody has to work for a trust; the trusts can keep men in so called hopeless conditions only so long as there are men who are too ignorant to know of the science of getting rich, or too intellectually slothful to practice it.

Begin this way of thinking and acting, and your faith and purpose will make you quick to see any opportunity to better your condition. Such opportunities will speedily come, for the Supreme, working in All, and working for you, will bring them before you. Do not wait for an opportunity to be all that you want to be; when an opportunity to be more than you are now is presented and you feel impelled toward it, take it. It will be the first step toward a greater opportunity. There is no such thing possible in this universe as a lack of opportunities for the man who is living the advancing life.

It is inherent in the constitution of the cosmos that all things shall be for him and work together for his good; and he must certainly get rich if he acts and thinks in the Certain Way. So let wage-earning men and women study this book with great care, and enter with confidence upon the course of action it prescribes; it will not fail.

STUDY GUIDE

The Advancing Man

1. This chapter opens with an assertion that whatever your vocation, in whatever way you wish to have abundance manifest in your life, you will come into such close touch with the Source of Life that you will be phenomenally successful. The example given was that of a physician becoming an extraordinary healer. Other than financial wealth, in what other forms would you like abundance to manifest in your life?

2. Wattles states that by applying the principles of faith, purpose and gratitude, an Advancing Man or Woman in medicine will "cure every curable case he undertakes, no matter what remedies he may use." This seems to emphasize then, that one's energy is the healer over their physical remedy. Do you believe this to be true? If so, why? If not, why not?

3. With reference to the clergyman, Wattles emphasizes that the world needs and will support a preacher who lives and demonstrates the science of life from the pulpit. Think back to the most powerful sermon or speech that you have ever heard. Why do you believe it held such power? Why do you believe the speaker was so powerful?

4. The teacher who lives the science of life will inevitably give the faith and purpose they possess to their students. Who was your favorite teacher? How did they affect you?

Why do you think they had so much more influence on you than others?

5. Wattles states that getting rich is an exact science, just like the law of gravity. You can experience his conviction in this assertion. It is the kind of conviction you need to support that which you desire to manifest into your life. With what you have read thus far in Wattles' book, why do you think his message has withstood the test of time?

6. Wattles suggests that you avoid working hard to please your employer. He emphasizes that doing so will not advance you. Do you find yourself trying to impress your employer?

7. Do you put your employer on a pedestal above you? If so, why do you think he or she is more powerful than you?

8. Putting others on pedestals disempowers both you and those individuals. How might you get your employer and others off of the pedestal that you put them on?

9. According to the author, being too large for your place in employment is not enough. You also need to:
   • Have a clear concept of what you want to be;
   • Know that you can become what you want to be;
   • Be determined to BE what you want to be.

   Reflect on your deeds and actions throughout the past month. How have you improved in each of the three areas? Provide examples of your progress.

10. Are there any areas where you think you need to gain more confidence?

11. Wattles suggests that you get your mind off of pleasing your employer and onto advancing yourself. How might you take the emphasis off of them and onto yourself?

12. The power of purpose should radiate from you to all who come in contact with you. Have you ever met someone who was extremely "on purpose"? Describe them and how they affected others.

13. If you are on purpose, others will be attracted to you, and if you cannot advance in your present job, an opportunity to take another job will arise for you. Do you concern yourself with "how" this will happen?

14. Make a commitment to forget about how, so that you can watch the magic of synchronicity take shape in response to your to faith, commitment, and gratitude. What do you feel when you allow yourself not to worry about "how" living your life's purpose unfolds?

15. According to Wattles, God cannot help helping you, and He must do so in order to help Himself. What do you think he means by this? How do you think helping you would help God?

16. Wattles points out that "If a few thousand of its employees would enter upon the Certain Way, the steel trust would soon be in a bad plight; it would have to give its workingmen more opportunity or go out of business." This is an interesting premise in that the consciousness of a mass of individuals could bring such a business down. Do you believe this to be true? Have you seen evidence of it in the business world?

17. In the final sentence of this chapter Wattles states, "Let wage-earning men and women study this book with great care, and enter with confidence upon the course of action it prescribes; it will not fail." Do you get an energetic surge from this statement? Does it fill you with a sense of hope and conviction? Read the statement aloud a few times, and then write about how it makes you feel.

18. It is interesting that Wattles has been dead for several decades, yet the power of his words is still so very strong and transformative. How does his strong conviction affect you and your sense of this system working for you?

Chapter 16

Some Cautions, and
Concluding Observations

Many people will scoff at the idea that there is an exact science of getting rich; holding the impression that the supply of wealth is limited, they will insist that social and governmental institutions must be changed before even any considerable number of people can acquire a competence. But this is not true. It is true that existing governments keep the masses in poverty, but this is because the masses do not think and act in the Certain Way. If the masses begin to move forward as suggested in this book, neither governments nor industrial systems can check them; all systems must be modified to accommodate the forward movement.

If the people have the Advancing Mind, have the Faith that they can become rich, and move forward with the fixed purpose to become rich, nothing can possibly keep them in poverty. Individuals may enter upon the Certain Way at any time, and under any government, and make themselves rich; and when any considerable number of individuals do so under any government, they will cause the system to be so modified as to open the way for others. The more men who get rich on the competitive plane, the worse for others; the more who get rich on the creative plane, the better for others. The economic salvation of the masses can only be accomplished by getting a large number of people to practice the scientific method set down in this book, and become rich. These will show others the way, and inspire them with a desire for real life, with the faith that it can be attained, and with the purpose to attain it. For the present, however, it is enough to know that neither the government under which you live nor the capitalistic or competitive system of industry can keep you from getting rich. When you enter upon the creative plane of thought you will rise above all these things and become a citizen of another kingdom.

But remember that your thought must be held upon the creative plane; you are never for an instant to be betrayed into regarding the supply as limited, or into acting on the moral level of competition. Whenever you do fall into old ways of thought, correct yourself instantly; for when you are in the competitive mind, you have lost the cooperation of the Mind of the Whole.

Do not spend any time in planning as to how you will meet possible emergencies in the future, except as the necessary policies may affect your actions today. You are concerned with doing today's work in a perfectly successful manner, and not with emergencies which may arise tomorrow; you can attend to them as they come.

Do not concern yourself with questions as to how you shall surmount obstacles which may loom upon your busincss horizon, unless you can see plainly that your course must be altered today in order to avoid them. No matter how tremendous an obstruction may appear at a distance, you will find that if you go on in the Certain Way it will disappear as you approach it, or that a way over, though, or around it will appear. No possible combination of circumstances can defeat a man or woman who is proceeding to get rich along strictly scientific lines. No man or woman who obeys the law can fail to get rich, any more than one can multiply two by two and fail to get four.

Give no anxious thought to possible disasters, obstacles, panics, or unfavorable combinations of circumstances; it is time enough to meet such things when they present themselves before you in the immediate present, and you will find that every difficulty carries with it the wherewithal for its overcoming. Guard your speech. Never speak of yourself, your affairs, or of anything else in a discouraged or discouraging way.

Never admit the possibility of failure, or speak in a way that infers failure as a possibility.

Never speak of the times as being hard, or of business conditions as being doubtful. Times may be hard and business doubtful for those who are on the competitive plane, but they can never be so for you; you can create what you want, and you are above fear. When others are having hard times and poor business, you will find your greatest opportunities. Train yourself to think of and to look upon the world as a something which is Becoming, which is growing; and to regard seeming evil as being only that which is undeveloped. Always speak in terms of advancement; to do otherwise is to deny your faith, and to deny your faith is to lose it. Never allow yourself to feel disappointed. You may expect to have a certain thing at a certain time, and not get it at that time; and this will appear to you like failure. But if you hold to your faith you will find that the failure is only apparent.

Go on in the certain way, and if you do not receive that thing, you will receive something so much better that you will see that the seeming failure was really a great success. A student of this science had set his mind on making a certain business combination which seemed to him at the time to be very desirable, and he worked for some, weeks to bring it about. When the crucial time came, the thing failed in a perfectly inexplicable way; it was as if some unseen influence had been work-ing secretly against him. He was not disappointed; on the contrary, he thanked God that his desire had been overruled, and went steadily on with a grateful mind. In a few weeks an opportunity so much better came his way that he would not have made the first deal on any account; and he saw that a Mind which knew more than he knew had prevented him from losing the greater good by entangling himself with the lesser.

That is the way every seeming failure will work out for you, if you keep your faith, hold to your purpose, have gratitude, and do, every day, all that can be done that day, doing each separate act in a successful manner. When you make a failure, it is because you have not asked for enough; keep on, and a larger thing then you were seeking will certainly come to you. Remember this. You will not fail because you lack the necessary talent to do what you wish to do. If you go on as I have directed, you will develop all the talent that is necessary to the doing of your work. It is not within the scope of this book to deal with the science of cultivating talent; but it is as certain and simple as the process of getting rich.

However, do not hesitate or waver for fear that when you come to any certain place you will fail for lack of ability; keep right on, and when you come to that place, the ability will be furnished to you. The same source of Ability which enabled the untaught Lincoln to do the greatest work in government ever accomplished by a single man is open to you; you may draw upon all the mind there is for wisdom to use in meeting the responsibilities which are laid upon you. Go on in full faith.

Study this book. Make it your constant companion until you have mastered all the ideas contained in it. While you are getting firmly established in this faith, you will do well to give up most recreations and pleasure; and to stay away from places where ideas conflicting with these are advanced in lectures or sermons. Do not read pessimistic or conflicting literature, or get into arguments upon the matter. Do very little reading, outside of the writers mentioned in the Preface. Spend most of your leisure time in contemplating your vision, and in cultivating gratitude, and in reading this book. It contains all you need to know of the science of getting rich; and you will find all the essentials summed up in the following chapter.

STUDY GUIDE

Some Cautions, and Concluding Observations

1. Wattles asserts that the reason that the masses are in poverty is not because the existing governing bodies keep them that way, but because they do not think and act in the Certain Way. This would especially make sense if you did not believe in "victim" consciousness. What have your beliefs been about mass poverty?

2. If your beliefs about mass poverty have differed from the author's, based on the new insights and information he has shared in this book, has your mind been changed?

3. If the masses begin to move forward, then all systems must be modified to accommodate that movement. Take some time to visualize a world of mass abundance consciousness, where thousands upon thousands are acting in the Certain Way. How would the world look? How would government be run? How would families and friendships be celebrated? How would theologies be honored? How would the earth be honored and maintained? Visualize all of this and more, using all of your senses to feel into the experience. After completing this visualization, write about what you experienced in as much detail as possible.

4. Do you realize that you just fed into raising the energy of the masses from lack to abundance simply by doing the

exercise in question #3? List three other ways in which you can contribute to raising the abundance consciousness of the world.

5. Those who commit to enter upon the Certain Way shift the existing system so that it opens the way for others to follow. By this example, you can see how committing to manifesting your own abundance is really an altruistic action on your part. In serving yourself, you serve the world. In what other ways have you pioneered or instigated change in your life (take care not to trivialize any such actions you've taken in the past)?

6. Getting rich on the competitive plane worsens things for others, while doing so on the creative plane, improves upon the lives of others. Do you believe you have ever improved upon the life of another? If so, how?

7. You should honor your commitment to personal growth, your courage to create change, and your purity of intention. Write a whole-hearted letter of praise and gratitude to yourself for taking this initiative.

8. Now write a heartfelt letter of praise and gratitude to you from the masses that you will touch by the choices you have made.

9. When you enter upon the creative plane of thought, you will rise above the competitive system and become a citizen of another kingdom. There is a sense of protection and reinforcement in this notion. On a scale from one to ten (one being "very little" and ten being "a great deal"), rate how much of the time you believe you run your life from the creative plane.

1———2———3———4———5———6———7———8———9———10

10. Are you ready to commit to changing that scale so that your commitment is even higher? If so, what are you willing to commit to?

1——2——3——4——5——6——7——8——9——10

11. What specific steps are you going to take to support your new commitment? List them.

12. Wattles cautions you not to fall into the old ways of thought. When you do, instantly correct yourself. What methodology have you put into place to pull yourself forward, when you catch yourself falling into the old ways of thought?

13. You should not anticipate how you will handle emergencies, obstacles or obstructions. You are instructed to live in the moment and deal with such issues only if they arise. Why do you think Wattles suggests this? Explain.

14. You are also encouraged to guard your speech and avoid speaking in a discouraging way. While this has been a tenet of the positive thinking movement for many years, many of us are unaware of how much we negatively speak. Ask your friends and family to point out to you when you do. Then be sure to thank them for efforts.

15. For the next three weeks keep a small note pad in your pocket or purse. Make note of each time you catch yourself speaking negatively. See if you can lower the number of times you speak negatively by the end of the third week.

16. When you or others catch you speaking negatively, immediately break the cycle with speaking aloud or to yourself, "Cancel, cancel." Then turn the statement around, using a positive framework.

17. Wattles warns, "Take care never to speak of the times as being hard, or of business conditions being doubtful." He claims they are never so for those immersed in the creative plane. If you haven't already done so, make a conscious choice to focus your thoughts, words and energy on the positive in the world and in your world, in particular. Take a few minutes to focus on all the good that is in your world and the world in general. Write about what you see, feel and experience as you do this exercise.

18. You will find your greatest opportunities arise when others are struggling through hard times and poor business. How might others' difficulties support you in your business or manifesting dreams?

19. Wattles wisely encourages you to see "evil" as only that which is undeveloped. This is a part of always speaking in terms of advancement. Do you think referencing evil in this context will raise your energy? If so, why?

20. You are also encouraged never to allow yourself to get disappointed. This can be a tough commitment to follow through on. We all have our down days and at times feel discouraged. Wattles states that this is where your faith comes in to play. Sometimes we simply need a stimulus to kick us into a more positive frame of mind. You may find listening to music you love, or watching an inspirational or humorous video may help you to snap out of your emotional funk. After learning all of this new information, is there something different you can do to pull yourself out of feeling hopeless or disappointed? Write down three things you can do to pull yourself back into focusing and faith.

21. Wattles encourages that when you act in the Certain Way and do not receive the thing you want, know that you will receive something better. Can you think of times during

your life where apparent failures ended up being even greater successes? If so, write about them. You may not have had such experiences because you were not behaving and thinking the Certain Way. Set the intention to experience such "even better" opportunities, have faith and gratitude that they will come to you, and write about them when they come your way.

22. According to the author, "When you make a failure, it is because you have not asked for enough; keep on, and a larger thing than you were seeking, will certainly come to you. Remember this." He asserts that if you fail, you have not asked for enough. If you were to allow yourself to dream even bigger, what would you desire? Write about it. Then have faith, focus, gratitude, and do your best at all you do. If you do this, like your desires, that what you manifest will also grow!

23. If you do not have the talent to do what you desire, but are continuing as the author has directed, Wattles asserts that you will develop the necessary talent. In what areas of your life would you like to become more talented? Do you believe that somehow these talents will grow in you, if you follow and believe in the process outlined in this book?

24. Maintaining full faith that you can accomplish something has greater weight than having knowledge, talent or experience in a certain thing. Wattles cites Lincoln as an example, being that he had no prior experience, talent nor knowledge of government, but through his iron will, commitment and perseverance, he grew to become one of the greatest leaders of all time. Research other prominent figures in history that had little previous talent, yet grew to become outstanding in their fields. Write a brief summary about at least three such figures.

25. Do you believe that in some form or another that these great figures incorporated the principles and practices that Wattles outlines in this book? Describe.

26. In the final paragraph of this chapter, Wattles suggests that you give up most recreations and pleasure. He suggests that you spend most of your leisure time contemplating your vision, cultivating gratitude and reading his book. On a scale from one to ten (one being "very little" and ten being "a great deal"), rate how much of your leisure time you spend envisioning your desires.

1———2———3———4———5———6———7———8———9———10

27. Are you willing to give up most of your leisure time to practice this technique? On a scale from one to ten (one being "very little" and ten being "a great deal"), rate how much of your leisure time you are willing to spend following Wattles' suggested practices.

1———2———3———4———5———6———7———8———9———10

28. What do you believe the cost to be to you if you don't?

Chapter 17

Summary of the
Science of Getting Rich

There is a thinking stuff from which all things are made, and which, in its original state, permeates, penetrates, and fills the interspaces of the universe. A thought in this substance produces the thing that is imaged by the thought. Man can form things in his thought, and by impressing his thought upon formless substance can cause the thing he thinks about to be created.

In order to do this, man must pass from the competitive to the creative mind; otherwise he cannot be in harmony with the Formless Intelligence, which is always creative and never competitive in spirit. Man may come into full harmony with the Formless Substance by entertaining a lively and sincere gratitude for the blessings it bestows upon him. Gratitude unifies the mind of man with the intelligence of Substance, so that man's thoughts are received by the Formless. Man can remain upon the creative plane only by uniting himself with the Formless Intelligence through a deep and continuous feeling of gratitude.

Man must form a clear and definite mental image of the things he wishes to have, to do, or to become; and he must hold this mental image in his thoughts, while being deeply grateful to the Supreme that all his desires are granted to him. The man who wishes to get rich must spend his leisure hours in contemplating his Vision, and in earnest thanksgiving that the reality is being given to him. Too much stress cannot be laid on the importance of frequent contemplation of the mental image, coupled with unwavering faith and devout gratitude. This is the process by which the impression is given to the Formless, and the creative forces set in motion. The creative energy works through the established channels of natural growth, and of the industrial and social order. All that is included in his mental image will surely be brought to the man who follows the instructions given above, and whose faith does not waver. What he wants will come to him through the ways of established trade and commerce.

In order to receive his own when it shall come to him, man must be active; and this activity can only consist in more than filling his present place. He must keep in mind the Purpose to get rich through the realization of his mental image. And he must do, every day, all that can be done that day, taking care to do each act in a successful manner. He must give to every man a use value in excess of the cash value he receives, so that each transaction makes for more life; and he must so hold the Advancing Thought that the impression of increase will be communicated to all with whom he comes in contact.

The men and women who practice the foregoing instructions will certainly get rich; and the riches they receive will be in exact proportion to the definiteness of their vision, the fixity of their purpose, the steadiness of their faith, and the depth of their gratitude.

The End

STUDY GUIDE

Summary of the Science of Getting Rich

1. A thought in the substance from which all things are made produces the thing that is imaged by the thought. In other words, if you imagine something enough, it will materialize. This being the case, reflect on how you treat yourself. Do you judge yourself harshly when you are not "on task"?

2. If you imagine something enough that it materializes, then how do you believe judging yourself manifests into form in your life?

3. Does judging yourself serve your highest good or the highest good of the world in any way?

4. Have you focused your energy on compassion and patience with yourself? If so, how? If not, how might you begin to cultivate self-acceptance, compassion and honoring of your efforts?

5. How do you think feeling compassionate, patient and respectful of yourself manifests in physical form in the world?

6. Next time you find yourself in the competitive mind, as opposed to being hard on yourself, fill yourself with loving compassion and acceptance. Make note of how you feel after doing so. Compare this with how you feel when you belittle or judge yourself. Which serves your accomplishment of achieving your dreams the most?

7. Do a final exercise of gratitude. Through a prayer, declaration or symbolic expression in the form of collage, song
   or whatever else you may desire to create, acknowledge
   Wattles for his wisdom and guidance, express appreciate
   to the Source for the perfect co-creation of your life, and
   finally congratulate yourself for taking the initiative to read
   Wattles' book and to do this manual. Your life has been
   forever changed!

Printed in the USA
CPSIA information can be obtained
at www.ICGtesting.com
JSHW012032140824
68134JS00033B/3023